How to Change the Way You Look at Things (in Plain English)

Adam Khan
with Klassy Evans

ISBN-13: 978-1623810108
ISBN-10: 1623810108

Published in the USA

YouMe Works Publishing

DEDICATION

The way things look to you has a lot to do with the way you look at things. This book is dedicated to you. I hope you gain a newfound flexibility about the way you look at things so your life gets better, and you become even happier and more effective than you are already.

CONTENTS

ACKNOWLEDGMENTS

Too many times to count, we have been down, disheartened, upset, discouraged or angry, but then we created a new perspective and changed our feelings entirely and immediately. We'd like to thank all the teachers who helped us learn about how to do this "perspective magic." We would especially like to acknowledge two masters at shifting perspectives, Richard Bandler and the late Milton Erickson.

INTRODUCTION

In the movie, *The Game*, Michael Douglas plays Nick Van Orton, the wealthy son of a wealthy man. The story begins when Nick's brother (Sean Penn) gives Nick a birthday present: A life-changing experience, a personal-growth workshop, except it doesn't take place in a classroom — it takes place in your *life*, and you never know who is an actor and what is real. The game is especially tailored to you and you never know for sure what is staged and what isn't.

The creators of the game make Nick's well-ordered life completely fall apart. All the things he identifies with — his money, his calmness, his place in society, the order and predictability of his life — are taken away from him. His life as he has known it is destroyed one piece at a time.

When Nick tries to find out if this is all part of the game, it appears that the company was a big scam, stole all his money, and left town. They very realistically give Nick the impression they took him for everything he was worth. He lost his mansion, his credit cards, his Swiss bank accounts. He was suddenly penniless.

While all this is going on, we (the people watching the movie) don't really know what the truth is, and we see Nick going through all these miserable experiences and on the one hand we're seeing it as anybody would — just as miserable experiences and nothing more — and at the same time we are viewing it with the question, "I wonder if this is the perfect experience to teach him to be happier?" Because we realize these experiences are teaching him against his will to care more about people, to appreciate what he had, and for the first time in the movie, we feel he is actually *engaged* in his life. He looked deeply bored with his predictable life before the game started.

He was a snob who lived in a bubble and did not really experience real life or real connections with anybody. He needed nobody. But now he has no money, and he has to rely on the kindness of a waitress in order to get something to eat.

Is this a humbling experience, a beneficial, potentially life-changing experience for Nick? Or is it merely tragic misfortune? We, the viewers, don't know until the end of the movie.

Watching the movie was a great demonstration of a profound fact: That the same experience can be seen in at least two different ways, both of them equally valid. One way of looking at it only makes you miserable without any benefit. The other one *helps you learn* — to be a better person, to have better values, and to be happier.

And of course, the thinking viewer will also eventually realize while watching the movie, that *all of life* is like this.

Someone might get an ulcer, and that is clearly just a hassle and he has to take medication that gives him dry mouth or whatever...or...this is an indicator-beacon that says *change your life — the way you live produces too much stress.*

With the first viewpoint, he just feels frustrated and that probably just makes his ulcer worse. The ulcer itself becomes another stressful thing to add to all the other stressful stuff in his life.

With the second viewpoint, however, he may feel motivated to change his life in ways that'll make him happier in the long run.

The second viewpoint, the better one, the one that doesn't come naturally to anybody but the most buoyant optimists, is a *reframe*.

The point of view you have about something is like a frame around a painting. You can put any painting in a cheap cardboard frame and it looks like nothing special. Or you can put it in a well-made, museum-style frame that helps set off the painting, and it has an entirely different feel. Also, a green frame tends to bring out the green in the picture. The frame can really change what you see and how you see it.

Reframing means seeing the same situation in a different way. It means seeing the same picture through a different lens. It means seeing the same event in a different context. It means interpreting a situation in a different way — ideally in a way that makes things better — reinterpreting an event in a way that helps you feel better and deal with the circumstances more effectively.

We automatically see (interpret, understand) the events in our lives in a certain way. In my book, *Antivirus For Your Mind*, you learn that it really helps to scrutinize the way you naturally explain setbacks and to try to find mistakes in your explanations. You look at your explanations and ask, "Is it true? Is it accurate?"

But sometimes *you can't answer* that question. Either you don't know or the answer cannot be known at all. For example, if I think I lost my job because I have bad luck, is that true? Is it accurate? There is no way to know. Or if I explain the pain in my knee by thinking "I'm getting old," is that true? Is it accurate? Is that really the cause? Is it the *only* cause? Should we settle for those points of view about the setback that come naturally? Or should we reframe them?

That depends on what they do for us.

If an explanation or interpretation is making you unhappy and it doesn't help you deal with the situation well, that's a good place to use reframing.

You *must* explain events. You *must* have a point of view. If you don't do it deliberately, your brain will do it automatically. What explanation should you use? When you don't know whether an explanation is true or false, what *criteria* should you use?

The only intelligent criteria to use in that case is, "How *helpful* is it?" Does your explanation or point of view help you feel better and get more done, or does it make you feel worse and hinder you from doing what you want to do?

If you find your explanation isn't either true or false (either you can't find out or there is no objective way to decide), and it is definitely *not* helpful, unfortunately, you can't just leave it at that. You *have to* come up with another explanation or interpretation. Your mind will not allow "no explanation."

Your explanation can certainly be *provisional* — good until something better comes along, like a scientific theory — but you'd better *choose* your best interpretation or your brain will do it for you, and the way your brain does it automatically may not be in your best interest.

This book is about how to change your perspective. Since you would probably be most likely to want to change your perspective when things are going badly or you're not feeling great, the best way to use this book (after you've read it through once) is to keep it around and when things are going badly or you're upset or discouraged, pull the book out and browse it. Each chapter here can be read independently. So browse the book until you land on something that seems like it would help and use it right there.

After doing this many times, you will get pretty good at changing your perspective and will need to refer to the book less and less often.

Our hope is that once you're good at changing your perspective, you will help others learn how to do it too. It is a gift that keeps on giving.

Among many other benefits, becoming better at changing perspectives will help you and other people in your life develop that special quality known as inner strength.

THE CREATION OF
INNER STRENGTH

One kind of reframing is making plausible interpretations that help you. When you realize the first explanation you make of an event isn't a good one, ask yourself, "What would explain this event equally well — but make me feel better or make me more capable?" We're looking for a *strong* explanation of the event. Ideally you want your explanation to motivate you or energize you, or *at the very least* not bring you down.

For example, I found a great reframe in the book, *Pain Free: A Revolutionary Method for Stopping Chronic Pain.* Most people, when they experience pain in their body, think they need to *rest.* This is a good first response to an acute injury.

But if the pain becomes *chronic,* some people continue with this thinking, and the author, Pete Egoscue, says this is a mistake. When pain is chronic, it is caused by what he calls "motion starvation." This is an explanation for the cause of chronic pain. I had never thought of that as a possible cause before.

In other words, the human body *needs* to move in a variety of ways. Modern life doesn't require much variety in our motions, so we often go days at a time with very little motion variety (we go from sitting at a desk, to sitting in our car, to sitting in front of the television, to sitting in front of a computer), and what movements we do are in a narrow range. Over time, this *motion variety deprivation* causes pain.

Egoscue, in other words, *reframed* the cause of chronic pain. Rather than the usual explanations (such as, "if you're in pain you should rest" or "I guess I'm getting old" or "this must be an old football injury") he says the pain is caused by *motion starvation*, and the solution is more movement and a greater *variety* of movement.

This reframe, this entirely different way of looking at the same thing (chronic pain), would cause the opposite kind of behavior.

The question is, of course, which frame is correct? We now have two different explanations for chronic back pain. Do you know which is the best way to look at it? If you've got chronic back pain and you've just learned about this reframe, you really don't know if it's a better explanation or not, do you?

To find out which explanation is better, you'd need to find out which one has the better *result*. I've tried both explanations and the "motion starvation" explanation is the better one in my experience. Resting increases chronic pain; motion variety decreases it. It is a better way to look at chronic pain. This perspective leads to less pain. It can, in fact, make the pain disappear altogether.

A good reframe is a *strong* explanation of the situation — a way to reinterpret the situation so you are more effective, so you're more likely to get the results you want.

Reframing is a *skill*. It's something you can improve. You can get *better* at reinterpreting events. And it is an incredibly helpful, creative, and *practical* skill to have. The better you get at it, the more often you'll feel better, and the more effective you will be in the world.

THE ULTIMATE TEST

At one point in WWI, two million Allied soldiers were ordered to stop retreating and go on the offensive. This new battle had been raging for two days when Marshal Foch sent his general this famous message: "My center gives way. My right recedes. The situation is excellent. I shall attack."

Foch had been in command of the center of the whole line, and his renewed offensive essentially saved Paris.

He reinterpreted dire circumstances as a perfect opportunity, and we can now see, *after* the fact, that his interpretation was a *stronger* one (more effective, more likely to get the result Foch wanted) than the most natural one that would occur to most people in similar circumstances (namely, "we're completely screwed; run for your lives!").

Military situations lend themselves to legendary moments such as these, when all seems lost, when troop demoralization means certain and final defeat.

Morale is often the crucial deciding factor in military engagements (and in your own life).

In the 1950s Marines were completely surrounded by the Chinese in Korea (at Chosin). Someone asked Col. Lewis "Chesty" Puller if he realized they were outnumbered and encircled. "Those poor bastards!" he replied, "They've got us right where we want 'em. We can shoot in every direction now."

How's that for a reframe? They could shoot in any direction and *be sure* of hitting the enemy because the Marines were surrounded!

Think about how that point of view would influence morale. If Col. Puller didn't have a record of success behind him, of course, his men might have thought he'd lost his mind. But they knew he was an effective leader, and his attitude gave his men determination and fortitude. It was a strong interpretation of the situation. It made them more effective.

Contrast Col. Puller's reframe with the natural and automatic reaction, "We're completely surrounded and outnumbered. Oh my God! We're gonna die!"

The soldiers *didn't know* if they were going to die or not. It might have been likely, but that doesn't make it inevitable. So this is a perfect situation for a reframe because you can't determine the truth or falsity of any guess about the future. The only valid criteria for interpreting the event in those kinds of circumstances is to ask, "What will help us be more effective?"

One point of view that would *not* help is, "We're all going to die!" Col. Puller's point of view worked a lot better.

Let's look at another military example, this time from the Civil War. "Unconditional Surrender" Grant, as he became known during the war, often saw apparently bleak circumstances in a way totally different than his fellow officers. And this different way of looking was one of the most important keys to his legendary success on the battle-field.

Grant was once away from Fort Donelson when his officers and troops engaged in an intense battle, and when Grant returned, he found very low morale among his men.

When the Confederates attacked, they were carrying full packs on their backs. Nobody recognized the *significance* of that fact until Grant arrived on the scene. They were too demoralized to think straight.

Grant thought the only reason the Confederates would attack carrying packs is because they were trying to fight *to get away* rather than trying to win the battle.

In a dispatch, Grant pointed out that although his men were demoralized, "I think the enemy is more so."

He reframed the situation, in other words. He saw it from a different point of view than his officers. The Union troops were not merely demoralized and tired from the battle — they were fighting an enemy who was even more demoralized. And to Grant, that meant *whoever attacked now would probably win.*

Grant had enough evidence for either point of view: Either they were defeated...or they could attack again and probably win. The question was,

"Which was the most *effective* way to see this? Which way would bring the best *results*?"

Based on what he knew about morale, Grant made his decision. He rode his horse along the line of his disheartened troops, yelling out that the Confederates were trying to retreat, and he urged every man to refill his ammunition pouch and get ready to attack.

Fort Donelson fell. It was one of the most significant Union victories of the Civil War.

In war, as in many other challenging endeavors, morale can make all the difference. And morale can be changed with a reframe. Demoralization can be transformed into steely determination and that is a powerful change to make on a battlefield (and in other difficult or challenging situations).

It was a particular talent of Grant's to generate his reframes by seeing things from the enemy's point of view.

War tends to create fear, of course, and fear tends to narrow your focus. Fear gives you tunnel vision. Soldiers often focused on their own dire situation and didn't see the big picture.

Have you ever had that problem? Next time, try reframing your "dire" situation and see what happens.

Grant was often able to reframe circumstances by widening his point of view, by bringing in more of the scene, and many times this broader point of view made it obvious that the circumstances were less dire than they seemed to a person with tunnel vision.

For example, it was pouring rain when Grant rode up to young Major Belknap, who anxiously told Grant that the Union troops were in trouble because of the rain. The roads were hopelessly muddy, bogging them down, and Confederates were close.

Grant replied, "Young man, don't you know that the enemy is stuck in the mud too?"

Major Belknap hadn't even *thought* of that. He had been so focused on the fearful and frustrating situation of his own troops, he'd forgotten that it was raining on the enemy too! His morale was immediately improved by this new reframe.

Try that next time you face an obstacle to your goal. *Widen* your point of view, and try to reframe the circumstances in a way that increases your determination.

We'll be going into more detail about *how* exactly to reframe circumstances. But first I want you to really grasp what a difference reframing makes in your ability to produce results.

BEHOLD THE POWER OF REFRAMING

Thor Heyerdahl would eventually become world famous as the author of *The Ra Expedition* and *Kon-Tiki*, but when he was much younger, he made a hundred-mile trek on skis across a mountain wilderness in Norway in the winter. On this trek, he discovered a way to boost his own morale.

Thor was challenging himself with a difficult task. But his adventure turned into a dangerous ordeal. A storm struck the mountains, blowing into a blizzard. The wind blew so hard, Thor had to lean forward almost horizontally to stay upright. His skis became so covered with ice he could hardly move them.

But Thor kept moving forward. He said to himself over and over, "This is the thing to turn a boy into a man."

He was doing just what Nick should have been doing in *The Game*. Thor was reinterpreting what was obviously a miserable experience. He reframed it into a transforming test of manhood. He reframed it into a rite of passage. And because of his reframe, he remained strong and determined. His reframe gave him strength.

A good reframe can give you tenacity and determination in the face of your challenges.

"Wise people," wrote M. Scott Peck, "learn not to dread but actually to welcome problems."

Do you know why that's wise? *Because you're going to have problems*. Guaranteed. If you welcome them and embrace the challenge, you will be better at solving them. And you will be less upset or depressed by problems when they come along.

Al Siebert, a researcher who spent 40 years studying the psychology of survivors of POW camps, survival situations, shipwrecks, etc., wrote, "One way guaranteed to increase your distressing experiences is to not want to be where you are. Your emotional distress decreases by deciding, like a flower seed, to bloom where you are planted."

Some people may naturally welcome problems because those people are lucky freaks of nature. The rest of us can *learn* to welcome problems by getting in the habit of framing problems as "opportunities in disguise." We can learn to welcome problems by deliberately trying to see what's *good* about the problem — by deciding right up front, "This is good," and then working to make it so.

I once lost a job because the facility I worked for suddenly closed. At first I was disturbed by my sudden unemployment. But Klassy and I decided right then we would make sure we would eventually be *glad* this happened. At that point, we didn't know what the future held, of course. So we chose a point of view that would help.

I took this point of view seriously — I really tried to think about how I could get myself a *better* job, and what that might be. I wasn't just thinking positively. I was determined about it, committed to it. I was going to *make sure* we were glad this happened.

And we were. I remember later realizing we had done what we set out to do: We were glad that old business closed. I found a much better job.

Any little trick you can use to help you think of problems as "good" will help. I remember reading about a business executive who would always respond to bad news with an enthusiastic "That's good!" And *then* he would seek to find what was good about it, or to *make* what had happened turn out for the best.

It might sound crazy, but his was a practical response to something that had already happened. He was very successful. No doubt, an important part of his success was his response to problems. With an attitude like that, you don't shy away from problems, you don't waste any energy whining about what happened, you don't waste any time trying to find someone to blame, and you keep your eyes open while you're dealing with it.

The funny thing is, after doing this several times (saying "That's good!" and then making sure you're glad the "bad thing" happened) you can actually say, "That's good!" with some confidence. You have confidence in *yourself* that you really *will* make sure you're eventually glad it happened.

SALES REFRAMING

Sales trainers often give their salespeople mental tricks to help them see rejections as not so bad, or even as a good thing. Do you think you'd have to be a nutcase to think that way? Let's say you're selling something door-to-door, and someone slams a door in your face. How could you possibly see that as a *good* thing?

That's a great question. And if you thought about it, I'm sure you could come up with a few ideas. And although at first those ideas might not make a salesperson feel any better, and the thoughts themselves would seem unnatural and unfamiliar, salespeople who succeed eventually learn to think that way, and it becomes as natural and familiar as the old way of thinking used to, and they no longer feel bad when people say no. They might even feel good!

One of the classic reframes of rejection used by salespeople the world over is, "This is a numbers game. If my sales record shows that one out of every ten people say yes, then that means the person who just said no brought me closer to the one who will say yes!"

Instead of seeing the rejection as a bad thing, a salesperson can actually (and legitimately) see it as a good thing. That rejection moved them one step closer to victory.

It's all in how you look at it. Reframing seems like an illusionist's trick or something superficial, but it is tremendously powerful, and people who get things accomplished in this world all learn to do it, consciously or not.

Richard Bandler, one of the co-founders of NLP (a school of communication and therapy), says when he was teaching college, he once had a student who complained his house was being bugged. Bandler's reply was, "What a chance to talk to these people."

Bandler gave the student other ideas. The student could play Milton Erickson tapes over and over (Erickson is a legendary hypnotherapist). Why not practice deep trance inductions and put the people bugging you into a trance and give them post-hypnotic suggestions?

Bandler didn't look for what was *wrong* with being bugged. He looked for a way to take *advantage* of it.

You can learn to have the same mental habit. Find the advantage and think of the "adversity" in terms of the advantage.

Milton Erickson himself was a master reframer. For example, when he was a therapist, a distressed young couple came to see him. Erickson talked to the wife alone first and she told him the whole sad story.

The man she married had been somewhat of a playboy, but on their wedding night, he couldn't get an erection for her. They had tried for two weeks now and he still wasn't able to do it. She was deeply hurt by this and she wanted an annulment.

But Erickson said, in essence, "But don't you see what a compliment this is to you? He is so overwhelmed by you, he isn't able to do what he was able to do with other women. *You are the overwhelming girl.* You go into the next room and think about that, and send him in."

The young man came in and *he* recounted the whole sad story. He was at the end of his rope. He didn't know what to do, or what was wrong with him. The young man said he finally found the woman of his dreams. She was beautiful. He admitted he had been somewhat of a playboy, having sex with many women. But he finally found his "one and only" and he was so happy.

On their wedding night, however, he couldn't get it up.

The young man was very upset by this. Erickson said to him, in essence, "Now you know she is truly the one — the one who has finally overwhelmed you. Don't you see? Nobody else has ever had this effect on you. You have found and married *the overwhelming girl.*"

Erickson then sent them home. By the time they got home, they were bursting to get into bed, they successfully had sex, and their problem was over.

Why? It was a classic Ericksonian reframe. Instead of an insult, which was one legitimate way to interpret his flaccid state, Erickson gave another and much more positive (and equally valid) interpretation, which took away her hurt feelings and took away the pressure on him, and then everything could work naturally without being impeded by her hurt feelings or his distressing (and therefore non-arousing) feelings.

Erickson's new interpretation wasn't necessarily more *true* than the old one, but it had more satisfying results.

This couple was on the brink of an annulment. Erickson's simple reframe changed the trajectory of their entire lives. And it was quick and almost effortless. *That* is the power of reframing.

Changing your perspective *can change your life.*

WHAT A DIFFERENCE

You can learn to be good at reframing, and it could really change your life *in the next week*. Not in some distant future. A reframe has an immediate impact. Your trajectory turns on a dime.

The biggest thing in your way is that when you experience a setback or a problem, you do not think of your interpretation as your "frame." You think of it as reality. So at first you will have to simply *assume* your point of view is only one of many valid possible interpretations, and then begin to come up with some alternatives. After you've done this a few times you will realize (if you haven't already) that *whatever* your point of view, it is not the only legitimate one possible. At that point, your mind is sufficiently open to begin generating reframes.

Think of something right now that is interfering with the achievement of an important goal. What's in your way? What is slowing you down? What do you think of as a *problem*?

Now sit down with a paper and pen and try to come up with ten reframes for that problem. If this exercise seems like "work," reframe it into a fun game.

First write down your frame for it now. "This is a problem," for example, or "This is a bad thing." Okay, that's one possible way of looking at it. Now come up with ten others. Make a list of ten different ways you could look at it.

To help you get out of your automatic or traditional way of viewing it, change your point of view. Think of someone you admire. How might *that* person look at your situation? How might the lead singer of your favorite band look at it? How might a successful executive look at it? How might an undersea explorer see it?

If you did this exercise every day, and nothing else — if you stopped right here in the book and never read anything else about reframing — it would change your life.

With daily practice, you would gain *a facility with reframing* that is extremely rare in this world.

PERSISTENCE AND DETERMINATION

It is highly likely that *most* survivors of harrowing ordeals, and *most* people who become very successful, are good at reframing. The ability to see things in a helpful way is one of the vital skills that can give a person persistence and the ability to endure. One *survivor* who also became very *successful*, for example, was Nelson Mandela. And, not surprisingly, he was good at reframing.

For example, when Mandela was a political prisoner in South Africa, many of the other prisoners he was incarcerated with were simply thugs. Mandela wrote, "I saw the gang members not as rivals but as raw material to be converted." And Mandela, in fact, recruited many of them to help in the cause (ending Apartheid).

He could have legitimately seen the gang members as bad people, dangerous, and viewed it as a terrible misfortune to be thrown in with men like those. Nobody would argue with that point of view.

But he saw these men through the frame of his goal. Instead of wishing things were different so he could accomplish his goal, he had the attitude, "How can I use circumstances *as they are* to accomplish my goal?"

That question can help you reframe your circumstances. When you use it this way, your goal becomes a lens through which you see the world, and it can reframe setbacks with the all-purpose question, "How can I use this to accomplish my goal?"

Mandela had dedicated himself to his mission. The South African government responded by cracking down harder and harder. Did that discourage Mandela? One possible way to see the situation was demoralizing: "The more we try, the harder they make it for us, so it would be best to give up. We can't win."

That way of seeing the situation is certainly valid, but of course, the goal could not have been achieved with that point of view.

Mandela had an attitude more like this: "I will fight until we have our freedom — jail, beatings, whatever I have to endure." He eventually reframed it this way: "The harder they suppress us, the more justified we are in fighting them. The more repressive the government, the more determined people will be to fight for their freedom." That's the same reframe Gandhi used in his effort to free India from Britain's colonization. The reframe gave their followers fortitude and helped them gain new converts.

Let me point out here that these reframes were not pulled out of a hat magically. Both of these men spent the time to *think*. They came up with many ideas and discarded most of them.

And when you have a challenge or difficulty or setback and you want to reframe it, take longer than thirty seconds to come up with something. Give it some thought. Come up with lots of ideas.

If you give it enough thought, chances are very good you will be able to find a potent reframe. That will change the way you *think* about it, which will change the way you *feel* about it, which will change what you *do* about it, and it'll make you more effective.

IT HAS TO BE *REAL*

If you've seen the movie, *Stand and Deliver*, you're familiar with Jaime Escalante. The movie is a true story about an immigrant from Bolivia who taught math at Garfield High — a run-down, dangerous ghetto school in East Los Angeles.

Most of Escalante's students' parents were immigrants from Mexico. These students felt they had no future and they couldn't care less about mathematics, especially *higher* mathematics.

But Escalante inspired a group of them to study for (and take) the AP Calculus exam — this is the Advanced Placement exam for higher mathematics — and most of them passed! The following year, even *more* of them passed. The next year, even more.

How did Escalante do it? He used a reframe to motivate himself to do "the impossible" against overwhelming odds.

The natural and automatic way to see the kids at this school was "They give me no respect, they are lazy, they don't pay attention, they don't care, they don't do their homework, they're not interested in school, the system is a disaster and works against reform, and the students will probably never amount to anything. I'll just go through the motions here and try to get moved to a better school."

That's the point of view many of the teachers had. Their demoralization was almost total. Escalante, however, saw the situation with a different frame. He thought, "I need to find a way to get their attention."

This is a *purpose* reframe. He wanted to teach math. He had quit the business world (he was an engineer) because he realized that what he really wanted to do with his life was teach. And these were the only students he had.

But to teach them math, he had to get their attention, so that became his focus. By focusing on that, rather than seeing their lack of attention as proof the kids were hopeless, their lack of attention was turned into simply *feedback* — "Okay, *that* didn't work. I wonder what else I could try?"

He saw it as a challenge. How can these kids be reached? His reframe motivated him to find innovative ways to teach. He saw the setbacks along the way through the frame of his goal — he wanted to teach and inspire these students, to show them the truth — that with hard work they might find a way out of their dismal surroundings.

And he succeeded. Many of his students went on to college and promising professional careers — almost a miraculous result in those seemingly hopeless circumstances.

MOTIVATION IS POWER

Reframing can make a huge difference by intensifying your motivation. And please understand, motivation is not just *nice*, it is tremendously powerful. What a person can do when sufficiently motivated is sometimes astonishing.

Sichan Siv, for example, came to the United States as a refugee from Cambodia. He barely escaped with his life. When the Khmer Rouge took control of Cambodia, it brought starvation and privation, slaughter, and hopelessness to the whole country.

Sichan's entire family was eventually executed (they were too educated — a crime punishable by death). Sichan was the only one of his family to make it out of the country alive.

In America, he worked hard. His first jobs were low-paying labor jobs, sixteen hours a day. And yet he was *glad* to do it. His positivity was not just lip service, he was very happy. He couldn't believe his good fortune! He was in America now and nobody was trying to kill him.

This is a *comparison* reframe, which you'll learn more about later in this book. On the one hand, sixteen-hour days are exhausting and difficult — especially scrubbing floors and washing dishes. Such long days of work would seem like torture to a lot of people. But compared to suffering and *actual* torture and death, and no prospect of a better future, the sixteen-hour days in America were *wonderful*.

His past (and his point of view) reframed the long, hard days into a privilege.

He eventually got more education and better jobs. For a long time, he had a little note posted above his desk that said, "The road to success in America is paved with hard work."

A good attitude and hard work tend to pay off, and Sichan eventually got a job as an assistant at the U.N. And then one day he got a call from the *White House* inviting him to become the first Asian refugee to ever be appointed as a ranking Presidential aide.

Sichan was able to work hard all those years and keep a good attitude, in part, because of his reframe. Instead of feeling bad because he had to work so hard, he felt *glad* to have the *privilege* of working so hard — and getting somewhere with his hard work.

Why did he feel good and work hard? Because thoughts produce feelings, and feelings produce action.

The thought, "poor me" produces negative feelings, which produce poor actions. The thought, "I'm fortunate to have the opportunity to work toward my goal" produces just the opposite.

But you can't just *say* "I'm fortunate." For a reframe to have any effect on your feelings, it must be genuine. If you don't believe what you're saying, it will have no impact on your feelings.

This is not a magic formula — it requires that you use your mind, not robotically repeat "affirmations."

You have to *really* look at your circumstances and think about them until you can come up with something real that makes you *genuinely* feel "this is good."

Years ago when I was working on the manuscript of a book, I often felt disheartened when it seemed to take forever, or there was too much material to work with, or organizing it seemed like a boggling task.

But one of the ways I reframed it worked well for me (because it was genuine): *Even if this book never gets done* — even if the worst case scenario happens and I die before it's finished — *I need to learn this material.* This reframed the job so I was more patient and persistent. I was more motivated during those times when the end result seemed very far away.

Since one of my strongest motivations is to learn, I was able to prevent myself from becoming disheartened by my automatic all-or-nothing point of view.

My reframe worked because it was *real.* I really did want to master the material and writing a book on the subject was a great way to do that.

CHOOSING HOW TO DIE

The movie and book, *Alive*, is the true story of two boys who *reframed their circumstances* and saved the survivors of a plane crash in the Andes mountains.

Nando and Cannessa had despaired along with their fellow survivors, hoping for a rescue that never came. So the two decided to hike out of the mountains themselves.

They had no cold-weather clothing, no hiking gear, they didn't know where they were, they didn't know how far they would have to hike, and they had very little food.

First they had to climb the enormous peak in front of them. The air was thin. The snow was deep. When they got to the top, they were completely exhausted.

They were hoping, expecting, praying that they would find green valleys on the other side (they didn't know how far west they were) but when they reached the summit to look beyond the mountain, all they could see were more snow-covered mountains stretching into the distance as far as they could see.

They fell to their knees, defeated. Crushed. It was over.

They were filled with hope as they climbed that first mountain, but when they saw the endless mountain ranges they would have to climb, they thought their chances of making it home alive were slim to the point of hopeless.

They were probably going to die in these mountains, they thought. It seemed pointless to continue hiking. But if they went back to the plane, they would be even *more* certain of dying in the Andes. If they stayed where they were, they would freeze to death. Their situation was a dire picture of hopeless despair.

After they got over the shock and horror, they made an important decision. If they were going to die in these mountains, at least they would die walking in the direction of salvation.

This was a reframe.

Instead of seeing it as an all-or-nothing goal, where failure was almost certain, they decided to view every step in the direction of civilization as a defiance against the odds. They would see each step as a triumph. The lives of their friends deserved their best effort. They would not give in. They would keep trying until they dropped dead.

Their ordeal was long and difficult, but they kept walking. They didn't give up.

Their decision to die walking to the West cast a new light on their suffering and kept their attitude determined even in the face of stupefying obstacles.

If they had stuck to the first and most natural point of view that came to mind, they would have demoralized themselves, they wouldn't have struggled on, and they would have given up. And they would have died on the mountain. And all their friends back at the plane would have died of starvation.

But that didn't happen.

Behold the power of a reframe.

OUR FINEST HOUR

Before the United States entered the second World War, Britain stood alone against what appeared to be an invincible German military machine. Hitler had annexed Austria and invaded Czechoslovakia, Poland, Denmark, and Norway, and then France capitulated. Britain stood alone.

There was no rational reason anyone could believe Britain would not soon be defeated. But here again we see the power of perspective. Winston Churchill talked to the British people, firing them up, bracing them for the fight ahead.

In one speech, Churchill said, "We shall not flag nor fail. We shall go on to the end. We shall fight in France and on the seas and oceans; we shall fight with growing confidence and growing strength in the air. We shall defend our island whatever the cost may be; we shall fight on beaches, landing grounds, in fields, in streets and on the hills." These were words of resolve and strength. But one of the things Churchill said in a speech is, I believe, one of the best reframes I've ever heard. It is uplifting and inspiring even now, more than a half century later, and I'm not even British. Churchill said:

> Let us brace ourselves to our duties, and so bear ourselves that if the British Empire and its commonwealth last for a thousand years, men will say: *This* was our finest hour.

Reframes can make themselves true. The perspective can so totally shift peoples' capabilities that what is originally declared *becomes* true. If you've ever seen a good documentary of what happened in the Battle of Britain, you will undoubtedly see that Britain's resilience in the face of Germany's onslaught was, in fact (at least up to now) their finest hour.

DIFFERENT WAYS TO CREATE REFRAMES

We've been exploring the power of re-frames to renew your motivation and strengthen your determination. Now we are getting to the nuts and bolts of *how* to create a good reframe. Three very good ways to reframe circumstances are to see them from another time, another place, or another person.

Viktor Frankl was a psychiatrist before he was sent to a Nazi concentration camp. While in the camp, he was severely underfed, he had to work in very cold weather with inadequate clothing, and all the while he witnessed unbelievable atrocities every day. It was more than many could take.

To ease his suffering, Frankl once recast his horrible surroundings into a different frame: He imagined when it was all over, he would give lectures on the "psychology of the concentration camp."

This reframe made his miserable situation look different. It gave him a certain distance from it, an objectivity, and he said it helped him maintain his resilience. It helped him endure. He looked at his present circumstances as though it was already in the past.

It also gave him a future to look forward to, and a reason to live. Frankl said, "It is a peculiarity of man, that he can only live by looking to the future…and this is his salvation in the most difficult moments of his existence, although he sometimes has to force his mind to the task."

Frankl survived the concentration camps and did, indeed, lecture about it later in his life. And sometimes in his lectures to psychology students he would remark on the strangeness and wonder of looking around at a lecture hall and realizing he was doing what he envisioned so many years before in the most dire circumstances one can imagine.

Frankl not only endured, but helped others endure by doing the same for them. He wrote later, "The prisoner who had lost faith in the future — his future — was doomed. With the loss of belief in the future, he also lost his spiritual hold; he let himself decline and became subject to mental and physical decay."

So that is one kind of reframe. Look at your circumstances from another *time*. Frankl found strength by looking at his circumstances from a time in the future.

When you're trying to come up with reframes, this is one way to do it. Look at your circumstances from the future or from the past.

The former head football coach for Florida State University, Bobby Bowden (who announced his retirement shortly after his 80th birthday) used a practical reframe during his successful coaching career.

He felt responsible for his players' actions, and sometimes needed to discipline them. "Long ago," he says, "I made up my mind not to make decisions based on public opinion. I never wanted anybody telling me how to discipline my players. I try to treat these players as I would my own children."

So he was coaching the team from the point of view of a father. He saw his situation from a particular frame, and he did it deliberately.

And he used the same frame *to help others* think differently. During an interview, he once said, "People write to me saying how a kid is a 'disgrace to the team' and that I ought to kick him off. I write back and ask, 'What if he were your son? What would you want me to do then?' Usually I don't get a letter back."

The point of view he adopted was that his players were like his children and he was like the father, and this point of view guided his actions successfully.

Lane Nemeth did something similar. She was trying to get a toy company off the ground and she ran into some typical business setbacks — debt, excess inventory, high interest loans. She was on the brink of bankruptcy. She was demoralized and thought about giving up.

But then she reframed the problem. "If this were my daughter," Lane asked herself, "and she were seriously ill, what would I do?"

Of course, if her ailing business was her child, she wouldn't even *consider* giving up. And it wouldn't matter how difficult it was, she would do whatever needed to be done.

And so she did what she had to do to save her business. She cut payroll. She got another bank to help. She stuck it out. And it worked.

Reframing her failing business as a suffering child of hers gave Lane the motivation to persist and succeed. It gave her the will to do what was necessary. It was difficult and sometimes her decisions were painful, but that is often what it takes to make something happen.

When you're coming up with possible reframes, try to look at your business or problem as a person or cast *yourself* in a different role — not just a business owner, but the mother of a sick child. Not just a coach, but a father.

HOW BAD DO YOU WANT IT?

Reframing the suffering *itself* is often a powerful generator of motivation. When Morgan Freeman was first starting out as an actor, for example, he struggled with the few acting jobs he could find, and the ones he found were flops. He made almost no money, and he would sometimes go days at a time without even eating because he just didn't have enough money to buy food. He worked in low-paying jobs to make ends meet.

A lot of successful people have stories of suffering, privation, long hours, and the seeming improbability of making it. How do they continue to press on? Have you ever wondered?

They understand that *this is what it takes.* That's how they do it. They ask themselves: "Do I want it badly enough?"

In other words, instead of "poor me, I suffer so," it's more like, "everybody wants to be an actor, but I'm willing to work harder and suffer more than my competition if that's what it takes to make it."

The movie, *As Good As It Gets,* had lots of great lines, but there was one in particular I've used many times on myself. Melvin (Jack Nicholson) is thinking about going to visit Carol (Helen Hunt) and tell her how he feels about her, but he's very nervous. He really wants to go, but he's scared.

He's talking to Simon (Greg Kinnear). Simon says to Melvin (giving him a pep-talk): "You can do this, Melvin! You can do this."

Melvin says, "She might kill me if I go over there."

Simon's comeback is a classic. "Well, then get in your jammies and I'll tell you a story!"

I've said that line to myself when I was thinking about avoiding some suffering (inconvenience, effort, privation, anxiety, embarrassment, rejection, or hardship) for the sake of an important goal.

The line reframes the "problem" doesn't it? It actually frames it as a challenge — do you want it or not? Do you want everything handed to you on a silver platter, or are you willing to do whatever it takes to get what you want?

For Melvin, who really loved Carol, the question was, "Do you really want her? And if you don't want her, if you'd rather play it safe and live without her, if you'd rather live out your days always wondering what *might* have happened if you had mustered a little more courage, then get in your jammies and I'll tell you a story!"

The unsaid part is: "But if you're willing to risk being embarrassed or rejected, if you're willing to suffer to get what you want, then stop all the fretting and hand-wringing, and get moving!"

That's a great reframe. You will get a lot farther in this world if you would simply be more willing to suffer for the cause — to see the "suffering" as legitimate and worthy and necessary to get what you want.

I'M NOT DESIRABLE

I know a woman who wanted to get a job in the accounting department of a large firm — a job she had the education and experience for. She sent out eleven resumes and heard nothing back. She gave up on the idea and kept doing what she was doing — something she didn't really like (selling computers).

She was hurt by the lack of interest. She thought she had something to offer these firms. The way she put it was "I was under the delusion I was desirable." The lack of response told her otherwise, or so she thought.

And sure, *one* way to interpret the lack of response is to think, "I'm not as desirable as I thought."

But what's *another* way? What's an alternative explanation for this setback? How would *you* reframe it? I'm sure you can think of literally hundreds if I gave you enough time — hundreds of other ways to frame this event that are all at least somewhat plausible.

We're not talking about *facts* here. She doesn't *know* the facts. She doesn't know why there was a lack of response. So her interpretation of it has to be based on something else besides accuracy.

Because she doesn't really know, her interpretation should be based on *what will serve her.* The first explanation she made — the one that popped into her head and she felt stuck with — didn't serve her. Thinking she was undesirable made her want to crawl back into her shell and never venture out again. The interpretation didn't help her get what she wanted.

One of the traps of negative emotions is they make you narrow-minded and uncreative.

In a better mood, she would see there are other possible explanations. But the explanation she came up with first was so depressing, she was unable (without the knowledge or ability to reframe her circumstances) to think of something else.

As you can see, a reframe would really help her. She would be better off if she could see the same event in a different frame, a frame that would prevent her from feeling bad, a frame that would motivate her to keep striving for her goal. In this case, she wanted a better job in a field she liked.

I came up with a few ideas off the top of my head. She could look at her rejection in any of the following ways and she would have more motivation to pursue her goal, more energy, more creativity and power, and she would feel better. The lack of interest from those companies might have been because:

- **Her resume needs to be improved.** This explanation could motivate her to learn more about resumes, or hire a resume consultant, or just spend a few weeks making it as good as she could.

- **She didn't show up in person.** This reframe would encourage her to show up in person and at least *find out* if that makes a difference.

- **They already get hundreds of resumes every week.** They don't even bother looking at one until an applicant shows up at least three times — this weeds out the ones with only a weak desire. This interpretation would motivate her to try much harder, to remain determined and to *keep trying*. Her first response, her natural, automatic response only made her want to give up.

- **Maybe she doesn't really want to be an accountant.** Maybe her heart isn't in it, and this was a lucky coincidence that she didn't get any interest from these companies. This would motivate her to give it some thought. Is she *sure* this is what she wants to do? And if she gave it some thought and decided the answer was *yes*, she would feel more motivated because she clarified her goal. If she found out she really *didn't* want to do it, she would be free to find something she cares more about.

- **Maybe the lack of interest is only because of the season.** Maybe at this time of year, they don't hire new people. This would motivate her to find out when is the best time to

apply, and while she's at it, she
could try to find out what is the best
way to apply.

I could go on and on, coming up with reframes. Any of these and any of hundreds more would be useful interpretations to make, and would motivate further action. And any of them are better than the demoralizing point of view that came naturally to her.

As it turns out, the real explanation was: *Large corporations move slowly.* Shortly after our conversation, she got two calls back, long after she had already given up.

She had only worked in small firms before, but her recent resumes were only sent to large corporations. She didn't realize they moved so much slower.

Many people, of course, don't even get as far as she did — they're too afraid of feeling that kind of rejection so they wouldn't have sent out the resumes in the first place.

The good news is, you're probably not one of them. The bad news is: That means you're going to have to deal with rejection. Depending on what you want to do, you might have to deal with quite a lot of it. The way you reframe it will make a *huge* difference in how you feel and in how successful you will be eventually.

REJECTED WRITERS

Writers, for example, typically experience lots of rejection. The manuscript for the book, *Zen and the Art of Motorcycle Maintenance*, was rejected by over 120 publishers. That was in 1974. It is *still* selling well. I checked on Amazon 34 years later and its Amazon sales rank was 1,180[th] — out of *four million.*

When Dr. Seuss was in high school, his art teacher told him, "You will never learn to draw." In college, his fraternity voted him Least Likely To Succeed. His first manuscript, *And To Think That I Saw It On Mulberry Street*, was rejected by 27 publishers before it was accepted.

Danielle Steel has over 550 million books in print and she was in the *Guinness Book Of World Records* for having eleven consecutive books on the *New York Times* bestseller list. But the first *five* novels she wrote were turned down and have never been published!

Clearly, each of these authors and many others with similar tales of rejection found a way to frame rejection in a way that didn't destroy their motivation to persist.

The ability to deliberately create constructive frames will help you no matter what your goal. For example, when I first started giving public speeches, I began at service groups like Rotary Clubs and

Kiwanis, and I was basically their twenty minutes of entertainment, and that's how the audiences seemed to feel about it. I didn't like that. I wanted them to listen *intently* and take it seriously. When they listened so casually, it was disheartening to me.

But I reframed the situation. I decided I would *make* them get how important this was. I came up with a lot of different reframes, but this particular reframe helped me the most.

At the time, my speeches were about the principles in *Antivirus For Your Mind.* I had seen the principles do great things for people and they had made a huge difference to me personally, and I'd be *damned* if I would let those people walk out of the meeting unmoved by them. I was determined to speak in such a way that they would *get* it.

Whenever I felt downhearted or discouraged or nervous about an upcoming speech, I would say to myself with feeling, "I will *make* them get how important this is!" And I said it to myself many times *while* I was speaking.

And I *did* get them to listen. I sometimes even yelled at them! I was impassioned and determined to get through to them, and they sat up and took notice. People would come up to me afterwards to tell me how much it meant to them.

I've used reframes in so many ways. For example, I sometimes run into people (or hear from them online) who are against my work, who feel that self-help stuff in general is nonsense, and that people are genetically predestined to be as happy or optimistic or depressed as they are, and it gives people "false hope" to tell them otherwise. Trying to help people become happier or more successful, they imply, is all just a big scam.

This used to feel demoralizing. My natural, automatic "frame" was: "I'm not appreciated." Or sometimes I thought, "There is just too much negativity in the world." And I felt negative emotions in response to these thoughts.

But I reframed it. "This is a noble struggle," I would say to myself, "People are suffering and feeling unnecessary negative emotions, and I know some things that can help them."

In my more dramatic moments, I would frame it more like this: "The forces of Darkness are enveloping the world and I am fighting the good fight. I'm fighting for the cause of sanity and health and happiness." You can read more about this in the chapter *What Myth Do You Live By?* (coming up later in this book).

Part of the way I reframed my mission was to think about the women who fought for the power to vote in America. Lots of people were fervently and belligerently against them in their struggle. It took more than *seventy years* of hard fighting for women to win the right to vote. It seems hard to believe now. It seems so self-evident that women should be allowed to vote. But it was a long and difficult struggle and people were against them.

And yet, isn't that what made their struggle noble? That it *wasn't* the popular thing but that it was *right?*

Happiness and optimism may not be popular but they are right and good and have positive, healthy, sanity-producing side-effects, not just for the person who is feeling better and getting more done, but for the other people in their lives — children, spouse, friends and family, people they work with — everybody is influencing everybody else, and someone who thinks better, who makes strong, healthy reframes about unexpected, seemingly unfortunate events helps others see things more sanely just by example.

Anyway, because I know all this, I have been able to successfully reframe negative responses to "self-help" and accusations of giving "false hope."

In case you don't know about the impact of your mood on others, I'll share with you a few tidbits to whet your appetite. You can learn more at Moodraiser.com.

MOOD MAKES A DIFFERENCE

Your mood has an influence on the moods of others. That means improving your own mood does something valuable for the people who know you. That means reframing your setbacks not only help you persist with your goals, it is good for the people you love.

Lots of research has been done on this. For example, using the voluminous data collected in the Framingham Heart Study, researchers looked at 5000 people over a period of twenty years. Many of the participants knew each other, so the researchers fed all the connections and their mood data over the two decades, and discovered something deeply heartening. Each person's happiness ripples out into others' lives.

In other words, your happiness — your good mood — causes a ripple of good moods to go out from you to the people you know, and the closer people are to you, the stronger the effect.

Here's another uplifting finding from the same study: *Good moods* have a greater ripple effect than *bad moods*. In other words, your good moods have more of a positive effect on others than your bad moods have a negative effect on them. And *their* good moods influence you more than their bad moods.

Here's something from an entirely different angle: Heart bypass patients who are married to someone who is anxious *are more likely to be depressed* even a year and a half after the surgery than patients who have more relaxed spouses, according to a study led by John M. Ruiz, PhD, assistant professor of clinical psychology at Washington State University.

And depression is particularly dangerous for people with heart disease, so this is a noteworthy effect.

A different study, this one on women, found that a woman's arteries are more likely to harden when her arguments with her spouse include expressed hostility.

I could go on and on. But the point is, your mood matters to the people around you. It is well worth your time to practice reframing negative circumstances so it improves your mood.

It also matters to your own ability to succeed. A study by Sonja Lyubomirsky, professor of psychology at the University of California, Riverside showed that "happiness is literally its own reward: It breeds success, just as success can breed happiness."

As the *New York Times* News Service put it: "While everyone knows that successful careers and relationships make people happy, new research suggests this process works both ways."

And your mood also affects your health, and again, there are lots of studies about this. One of them, considered the "most comprehensive" meta-study so far, found that when you feel good more often, your health is better and you'll probably live longer. The meta-study's lead researcher, Ed Diener, a University of Illinois professor emeritus of psychology, who is also a senior scientist for the Gallup Organization, of Princeton, N.J., said, "We reviewed eight different types of studies. And the general conclusion from each type of study is that your subjective well-being — that is, feeling positive about your life, not stressed out, not depressed — contributes to both longevity and better health among healthy populations."

A study at Yale found that a good attitude and a positive outlook can add an additional 7.6 years to your life. And here's an interesting perspective on that: It can add more years to your life than low blood pressure, which adds about four years.

Whenever something brings you down or makes you upset, try to see it in a different light. Try to reframe it in a way that makes you happier, that gives you strength, that boosts your fighting spirit, that makes you want to persist, and that helps you feel motivated and determined to accomplish your goals. It will make you feel better now, and it will also put into motion positive consequences that will ripple out into your life for a long time.

The first place to start when anything brings you down is the classic reframe — the subject of the next chapter.

THE CLASSIC REFRAME

This is almost a cliché: *It's a learning experience.* But it's a good reframe. This is an all-purpose, fall-back reframe in case you can't think of anything else, and it is almost always valid. You can gain some wisdom from almost any adversity if you are determined to do so.

Rather than waste time feeling bad or beating yourself up or lamenting your loss, this reframe boosts your resolve to change your future actions.

In their quest to survive the savage sea, Dougal Robertson had many "learning experiences." He and his family were adrift in the ocean after killer whales sank their sailboat.

On the fourth day on their inflatable life raft and little wooden dingy, they were all very hungry. Their sailboat sank so quickly, they were not able to grab much food. So Dougal was trying to catch a fish. He had a spool of fishing line aboard, a wire leader (to keep sharp teeth from biting through the line) and a lure. There were five people aboard and they were all very hungry.

Dougal cast his line out again and again, but no fish seemed interested. Then he saw three good-sized fish and excitedly cast in their direction only to see the spool, the line, the leader, and the lure all arc through the air and sink into the depths!

He had made a foolish mistake. He couldn't believe he'd been that stupid. That was the only fishing line they had! And that was the only lure they had.

But rather than wasting time beating himself up or lamenting his loss, he immediately determined never to make that kind of mistake again. It was a classic "learning experience" reframe.

"I resolved to examine every move before I made it," wrote Dougal, "and every decision before we acted upon it, for sooner or later, because I had overlooked something, someone would die."

A BETTER EXPLANATION

One characteristic of a good explanation is: *You can do something about it.* That's one of the best things about the "learning experience" reframe. If you explain your failed marriage with something like "women are heartless," it's not true and it's unnecessarily depressing, but more important for our discussion here, "women are heartless" is automatically disqualified as a legitimate explanation of a setback because *you can't do anything about it.*

In other words, if you come up with an explanation you can't do anything about, keep looking. Come up with something else because your explanation is worthless. It may *sound* good. And it may even be true, but if it doesn't help, keep looking. Find an explanation you can do something about.

For example, Hernando de Soto explained poverty differently than most of the experts, and because of his different explanation, he changed the lives of thousands.

It started one day as he stood on a bridge in a town in Peru. He could see two communities on either side of the river. One was clearly prosperous, with businesses and big houses. The other side of the river was completely different — no houses at all; only makeshift huts of cardboard, mud, and plywood. Each community had about the same number of people.

He was curious about this, so he talked with people on both sides of the river, trying to find out more. He discovered that both communities were founded by Latin American Indian immigrants — some on both sides were even originally from the same village.

Hernando's curiosity was fully aroused now. Why were these two communities so radically different? None of the usual (demoralizing) explanations seemed to apply. Here was a kind of perfect natural experiment that made it clear the usual theories *couldn't possibly explain* what was happening.

For example, one of the prevailing explanations for why Third World poverty is so pervasive in these regions is because *Indians are so communal*, free enterprise systems don't work with them.

Look at that theory. It is a theory you really can't do anything about, unless you wanted to try making Indians less "communal." It's a demoralizing explanation and if Hernando wasn't looking at the stark contrast of these two communities, it would be a hard theory to refute. But here they were, the same "communal" people, one group prospering, the other living in poverty.

Another, equally demoralizing theory is that "Yankee imperialists were exploiting the people." But again, the difference between these two groups could not be explained by that theory either.

Now Hernando just had to find out. He kept digging into the matter and found a man who had worked for over twenty years with the Housing Ministry for the area. The man was now retired. Hernando interviewed him, trying to get the full picture of how these two communities developed over time.

It turns out the two villages started the same way. Immigrants came and settled on land nobody owned. But the leader of one of the communities relentlessly pestered the government to grant them property rights. Eventually, the government gave each of the residents titles to the land they had settled on.

The people across the river never did that, and they *still* didn't own the land they lived on.

Now Hernando had a reframe — he had an entirely different way of looking at what causes chronic poverty. When people own their own land, they tend to develop it, to put down roots, to *invest* in their community, and to accumulate wealth.

When people don't own property, they have no incentive to invest or develop. Their "home" and possessions are all temporary. They could be evicted at any moment without notice and lose it all. Why would they build anything permanent or valuable?

This reframe created tremendous motivation in Hernando. Something could be *done* about it.

If simple ownership could make that much difference in the level of poverty, then he could help poor people rise out of their plight! He created the Institute for Liberty and Democracy. The institute has done experiments and launched grassroots campaigns. One campaign, for example, convinced the government to grant land ownership titles to tens of thousands of citizens.

Over the years, Hernando's original reframe changed the lives of many generations of people, and is still having an impact today.

HOMELESS TO HARVARD

Liz Murray's mother and father were drug addicts who didn't pay their rent and were eventually evicted from their apartment. Her mom was taken away to be treated for schizophrenia, alcoholism, and addiction to hard drugs.

Liz's father went to live in a shelter for the homeless. Liz was sent to her grandfather's, but he was abusive, so she went out on her own to live on the streets of New York City.

After her mother died of AIDS, Liz decided to complete high school. She had never really attended school.

She enrolled in an alternative school and completed four years of education in two years — and the whole time she was homeless! She kept her homelessness a secret from her teachers for two years.

When she turned 18, she wrote an essay to apply for a *New York Times* scholarship, and she won. She was accepted to Harvard University!

At the awards ceremony where she was given the scholarship, a reporter asked Liz, "How did you do this?" He was incredulous, amazed, and so was everyone else. What she did seemed impossible.

Liz didn't see it that way at all. "How could I *not* do this?" she asked. "My parents showed me what the alternative was."

In other words, one way to frame her life was: The poor girl had terrible disadvantages and basically no hope. She was given a raw deal in life, a terrible handicap, a wound that could never heal. Any dreams she had were only pipe dreams.

But she reframed her circumstances. After living a life like hers, she thought, how could she possibly be stupid enough to let herself suffer the same fate as her parents?

Her circumstances motivated her because she saw what happened to people who did not work toward positive goals.

Because of her reframe, her terrible circumstances actually became her advantage. It drove her on to accomplish what seemed impossible (at least to someone unaware of reframing's tremendous potential).

HOW CAN YOU USE IT?

When bad stuff happens, see if you can reframe it into an advantage. And if something happens you can't do anything about (or don't *want* to do anything about), change the way you interpret it so you feel energized and motivated.

When Arnold Schwarzenegger became governor of California, "He told Jim Lorimer that he liked nothing better than the feeling of living life on the outer edge of his energy and ability."

"Long before that," wrote Laurence Leamer in his book, *Fantastic: The Life of Arnold Schwarzenegger*, "if the Davis-backed bond issue was found to be illegal, the state would find itself in a fiscal crisis unprecedented in its history. Nonetheless, the governor was smiling — not a masked grimace, but an authentic expression of his emotions. He loved it when life was on the edge, and the difference between hope and despair no thicker than a dime."

Schwarzenegger has found a way to see challenges as something *desirable*, something he *likes*. It makes him feel genuinely good. He's not faking his good attitude. He has trained himself to reframe problems as opportunities, and has enough experience actually turning problems into opportunities that when a problem comes along, he genuinely feels good about it.

There is a big difference between this and someone who tries to appear "positive," who puts on a happy face, who tries desperately to believe that "everything happens for a reason."

Never try to make yourself believe something you really don't believe. This information on reframing is not *carte blanche* for thinking up and trying to believe imaginative nonsense. Find reframes that fit reality and that don't contradict what you know about the world. And, ideally, come up with reframes that make you feel *stronger*. This sometimes takes a little time.

One of the reasons "positive thinking" has a bad reputation in some circles is that people try to do it the *easy* way with phrases like, "Everything happens for the best."

That is an unthinking, all-purpose reframe that glosses over the ugliness of life, and doesn't change your feelings because you're pretty sure it isn't true. In other words, because you don't really believe it's true, it can't really make you feel energetic or motivated. It is just lip service.

Use your head, take some time, put in the effort, and make *good* reframes, and they can really and seriously change your life.

COMPARISON REFRAMES

In the book, A*drift: Seventy-six Days Lost at Sea*, Steven Callahan recounts his harrowing experience alone on a life raft. He lost 45 pounds during the trip suffered through extreme challenge and deprivation. His description of what it was like to be back on land gave me a new appreciation for something we all take for granted.

I'll give you a sample of his description in a moment, but first let's ask the question, *Why?*

Why did Callahan's *deprivation* make him appreciate something we usually take for granted? Because *taking something away* for a while forces you to compare your normal circumstances to something *worse*.

And here's the point: *What you're comparing your life to right now* determines how happy you are at the moment. This is a reframing principle you should make sure you never forget. The satisfaction you feel in your life right now is almost entirely determined by what you are comparing it to.

Sometimes people fast. That is, they don't eat for a period of time. I've done it myself for four days. One of the reasons people fast is that food is so amazingly delicious afterwards. Eating is almost like a religious experience. Why? Because eating is wonderful *compared to* not eating.

If you eat all the time, you really have nothing to compare it to, but after fasting, you can compare eating with not eating, and it makes eating one of the best things you've ever experienced!

When Callahan was found by three fisherman offshore after 76 days drifting in a life raft on the open ocean, they took him to their island in the Caribbean.

Once ashore, they drove him to a hospital in another town. On the way there, Callahan was *overwhelmed* with color and sound and smell.

While he was adrift on the ocean, he was surrounded for more than two months by nothing but blue sky and blue sea. He smelled nothing but the ocean and fish. Read his brief account of the car ride:

> We pass long stretches of sugar cane fields. Ox carts are piled high with cut cane. I cannot believe how sensitive I am to the smells of the cut vegetation, of the flowers,

of the bus. It is as if my nerve endings are plugged into an amplifier. The green fields, the pink and orange roadside flowers, practically vibrate with color. I am awash in stimuli.

The contrast between his life on the raft and normal life on land was intensely pleasurable. He appreciated colors and smells we just usually take for granted every day. *Why* do we take them for granted? Only because *they've always been there.* We haven't compared their presence with their *absence*.

During his voyage on the life raft, Callahan was soaking in the salt water sloshing into his raft for almost the entire time. So it was especially pleasurable to simply be dry.

When he got to the hospital, they cleaned him up and put him to bed. His description is *ecstatic.* Why? Simply because of the comparison between a small, cold, wet, abrasive, salt-encrusted life raft and a simple, ordinary bed:

I lay back on the sheets, clean sheets, dry sheets. I can't remember ever feeling like this before, though I imagine that I might have felt this way at birth. I am as helpless as a baby, and each sensation is so strong that it's like seeing, smelling, and touching for the very first time.

Comparisons. Your mind makes them all the time. And whether you feel contentment or dissatisfaction largely depends on what you are comparing your life to.

The problem is, we live in a culture where advertisers are constantly giving us perfect images to compare our lives with — perfect people with perfect homes and cars and spouses and children — and they give us the illusion that this perfection is somehow possible.

And it's not just an advertising problem. The advertisers are taking advantage of the way our minds work naturally. You automatically and naturally compare yourself and your life to others and to your own ideals and aspirations. In other words, without even trying, you habitually compare your life with something better.

Although the process of comparison happens without your active effort, you can assume control of it. Like your own breathing, it happens on its own, but you can make it do what you want at any time.

Why would you want to bother? Why change what you compare to what? Because it makes you feel better. And feeling better is good for you. As science writer Robin Lloyd put it after looking at the research:

People who positively evaluate their well-being on average have stronger immune systems, are better citizens at work, earn more income, have better marriages, are more sociable, and cope better with difficulties.

It makes a difference to feel better. And luckily, it can be accomplished without too much trouble. The feeling won't last for a long time, but neither does sleeping or exercising. The fact that the effect doesn't last is no reason to dismiss it. If you're willing to put in a little effort, you can feel a lot happier more often.

Here's one very simple and direct way to do it: When you feel discontented, ask yourself, "What could be *worse?*" And really try to think of something. You can always think of *something*, and it is usually pretty easy.

This is a reframe. Instead of looking at your life from the point of view of comparing it to what you would *rather* have, you're looking through a different frame. You're choosing a point of view just as legitimate: "What is this better than?" Or, "What would be worse?"

If you feel unhappy because you haven't advanced in your job as fast as you'd hoped, for example, imagine how you'd feel if you lived in a country or a time when advancement wasn't possible. Imagine being an "untouchable" in India, sentenced to generation after generation of poverty with no chance of escape for you or your children or your grandchildren. Imagine some real situations other human beings have experienced (or are now experiencing) that are much worse than anything you've ever had to endure.

Or you could remember when things were worse for *you*. That will change your outlook too. Instead of comparing your circumstances to your high expectations of yourself you haven't fulfilled, you can compare your circumstances to your memory of how things were when things were worse for you.

Try this technique and you'll recognize that in many ways you're lucky to be where you are and who you are. And this is not an illusion. It is a fact, and recognizing and acknowledging this fact gives you a good feeling.

It won't last very long, but it doesn't take much time or effort, and you can always do it again. The technique works every time, and you are rewarded every time.

In a way, it is a good thing the feeling doesn't last because as wonderful as contentment is, motivation is also wonderful. Striving for a goal — physical fitness, self-improvement, financial success, whatever — is practical and worthwhile. But when you want to feel some contentment, if you want to ease your stress, feel some relaxation, and enjoy being alive, take a little time and think about how your situation *could* be worse, or think about what *others* have gone through, or think about how your situation *used* to be worse.

To help you find some real situations you can compare your own life with, read books like *Endurance: Shackleton's Incredible Voyage*, *The Long Walk: The True Story of a Trek to Freedom*, and *Alive: The Story of the Andes Survivors*. Their difficulties will help you see your own life with new eyes.

REFRAME EXPERIMENT

In one of the most simple and elegant experiments I've ever read about, people were asked to complete the sentence, "I'm glad I'm not a..." They completed the sentence five times.

After doing this simple exercise, they were happier with their lives. Their "life satisfaction" was improved from the exercise.

Another group of volunteers were asked to complete a different sentence: "I wish I were a..." After this exercise, they were *less* satisfied with their own lives.

You have a lot of control over what you compare your life to, and if you would like to feel good more often, it behooves you to consciously exercise your control.

Another experiment looked at comparisons in a different way. A group of women were shown pictures of difficult living conditions from a hundred years ago. Another group were told to imagine and then write about what it would be like to experience a horrible tragedy like getting disfigured or terribly burned.

Afterwards the women filled out a rating scale to measure their satisfaction with the quality of their own lives.

Both groups were more satisfied with their own lives after the exercise. Why? Because it gave them something worse to think about and they naturally and automatically compared their own lives to it, and felt fortunate.

You can do a comparison experiment at home. Fill one bucket with ice cold water and another bucket with very warm water. Fill a third bucket with room temperature water.

Now soak one hand in the hot water and one in the cold water for a couple minutes. Then pull them both out and plunge them into the room temperature water. You'll get the strange sensation of the same bucket of water feeling both hot and cold at the same time.

Compared to the hot water, the room temperature water feels cold. Compared to the cold water, it feels hot. Comparison makes the difference. It influences your direct perception of reality.

In his autobiography, *Long Walk to Freedom*, Nelson Mandela describes his time in prison. It was pretty bad. Sometimes he was put in isolation where the only food he got was rice water three times a day. Rice water is the water rice has been boiled in. That's it. That's all he was given to "eat."

When isolation was over and Mandela was back in the normal prison, the tiny amount of horrible food they usually ate seemed like a *feast.*

I like to read true stories of survival, as you can probably tell. One of the reasons I like to read them is that I feel so fortunate when I'm done reading. I get up and go about my day, freshly aware that I am not starving or freezing or dying of thirst, and it makes me feel rich and lucky and satisfied with what I have.

I like it when authors use examples to illustrate a point, and I hope you do too, because I have another one for you: After returning to base camp from an arduous, intense brush with death in another true survival story, *K2: The Savage Mountain*, the authors wrote about how relaxing and wonderful it was to be back in base camp:

> At that moment we craved no delicacies, no entertainment, no luxuries. We felt like swimmers from a capsized boat who had

just completed the long swim to shore.
Merely being there was unspeakable luxury.

I really like that last sentence. Merely being there was unspeakable luxury. What is luxury? It is something wonderful you're not used to. What a rich person in New York City is used to would seem an "unspeakable luxury" to a poor person in a slum in Calcutta, India.

In studies on happiness, this issue of *luxury* is thrown into sharp relief. The researchers find that after having enough money to supply yourself with the basic necessities, money doesn't have much of an impact on your happiness level. People who are very wealthy are only slightly happier than people living modestly.

But there is an exception to this rule: If someone with a low income comes into frequent contact with people with higher incomes, it can make the lower-income person unhappier with his circumstances.

People who are very poor in, say, a remote village in India, can be pretty happy when everyone else in their village is also very poor. But a poor person in Beverly Hills (who actually would be rich compared to the person in the poor Indian village) might be miserable because he is comparing himself to all the people around him who have so much wealth.

When Sichan Siv escaped Cambodia during the Khmer Rouge bloodbath, his escape was very difficult and took a long time. When he eventually made it to the United States and got a job at the Friendly Ice Cream restaurant, washing dishes, mopping floors, and taking out the trash for 16 hours a day — he was very happy. Why? It's the comparison. He felt like the luckiest man alive. "I'm free!" he thought, "Nobody's trying to kill me!"

Those of us who grew up in the United States would find his situation — working at such a hard job 16 hours a day and making so little money — almost intolerable because we are comparing it to our own lives.

But we are not stuck only making comparisons that come naturally. You can deliberately make any kind of comparison you want, and the comparisons you choose really make a difference.

NAUSEATING COMPARISONS

An interesting study at Wake Forest University, where they seem to specialize in interesting studies, casts a new light on the whole subject of "positive thinking." Here's what they did: They gave volunteers "motion sickness" tablets. At least, that's what they told the volunteers. Actually, the pills did nothing.

Then the volunteers had to ride a rotating drum, something that tends to produce nausea in at least some people. Before the ride, the researchers told a third of the volunteers the pill would prevent them from getting nauseated. They told another third the truth: The pill was fake and wouldn't do anything. And they told another third the pill would actually make them feel *extra* nauseated.

They got on the ride. What do you think happened? Who do you think was the *least* nauseated? You may be surprised to learn it was the third group. They were expecting it to be bad, but it wasn't as bad as they thought. After the ride they were far less nauseated than the other two groups.

This is a comparison reframe again, and it reminds me of something that I once read about how to set up a joke or tell a funny story. Experts on comedy say that if you tell someone that a joke is *really* funny before you tell it, that joke better be *extraordinarily* funny. If you want people to laugh, you're better off saying, "here's a dumb joke." You set the expectations low so the joke seems funnier than it is by comparison.

The same thing holds true when you recommend a good movie. If you tell your friend it's the best movie you've ever seen, your friend's expectations are set really high. Your friend is more likely to enjoy the movie if you keep the expectations low.

This is also true for people. When you hear that a friend of a friend is a really great person or a big jerk, you're often surprised when you meet them. The really great person doesn't seem that great, and the jerk seems pretty nice. Your expectations were set ahead of time. You are comparing a one-sided, extreme characterization with a not-as-extreme actual person.

The principle is very basic but it has broad applications. The thing to remember is: *You can influence the frame* — the way something is perceived — by comparing it to something better or worse. And rather than making comparisons haphazardly and without awareness, you would be wise to choose your comparisons carefully so you frame things in a way that *helps* you rather than *impedes* you.

LOOKING INTO THE FUTURE

My wife, Klassy, creates and leads workshops for couples, where she puts couples through communication exercises. One of her most powerful exercises uses this principle of comparison and it has a tremendous emotional impact.

Klassy has each couple sit facing each other, gazing into each others' eyes, and she talks to them while wordless, beautiful music is playing.

"Imagine," Klassy says, "that at midnight tonight, your partner will die. Your mate's life will be over soon. Imagine how that would feel to you. The two of you have been through so much together..."

Of course, this is a very moving experience for almost everybody. Klassy gives them plenty of time to fully imagine this scenario and to feel how sad it would be.

"What would you miss the most about your partner?" Klassy asks, pausing for long periods so they can think about this while the music plays in the background.

Each pair silently continues looking at each other, pondering these questions, feeling the emotions, feeling what this person means to them.

"What special memories would you cherish?"

"What would you want to say to your partner before midnight?"

When they really can't take any more and the room is about two feet deep in tears, Klassy says something like this:

"Now imagine it is after midnight and your partner is gone. And realize how much you would wish your partner had not died and how badly you would want to be right here with your partner...to have your future still ahead of you..."

Long pause...

"And realize what you wished for has come true. The two of you are here, together, alive, your future ahead of you."

You've never seen so many people gaze at each other so totally in love before. "Now," says Klassy, "take some time and talk about your experience with each other."

The couples are always considerably affected by this experience. Here they are — like most couples — to some degree taking each other for granted, comparing yesterday with today, or whatever. Not really appreciating each other.

"You don't know what you've got till it's gone." Really? What if you imagined what it would be like if it was gone? Then realized it *isn't* gone? Guess what? You *can* know what you've got while you've got it! You can do it with deliberate comparisons. You can use comparisons consciously, and you can dramatically change the way you look at things.

This is a way to make positive events more memorable than negative ones. It directly counters the negative bias which makes you compare things in a negative way.

When people say, "count your blessings," they really mean compare your life to something worse, and feel grateful your life is the way it is. And it works. In one study, people who wrote in a diary about what they were grateful for only *five* minutes a day were *measurably* happier.

Five minutes! If you want to feel measurably happier, compare your present circumstances to something worse, or simply think about something you are grateful for. It is a simple reframe, and it'll never wear out.

No reframe will make you *permanently* happy. But you can reframe in many different ways, and you can do it as often as you like and it will almost always make you feel noticeably better.

HOW TO CREATE A REFRAME

If you can reframe a circumstance that makes you feel bad, you won't feel as bad any more. Nothing has changed except how you're looking at it, but that's enough to change your feelings.

For example, a few months ago I had to go to the dentist. I noticed I felt a little annoyed and nervous about it. I realized the "frame" I was using to interpret this event was: "I have to go do this unpleasant, inconvenient thing."

And my feelings were appropriate to that interpretation, as they always are. Your feelings always match your interpretation. I dreaded going and felt annoyed that I "had to" go.

So I asked myself, "Is there another way to look at this?" And instantly I realized that in most of human history, dentists didn't exist. People had horrible toothaches and there wasn't much they could do about it. Their teeth rotted out. Even a few hundred years ago, most of the "dentistry" consisted of pulling out a tooth that was causing pain (and pulling it out *without Novocaine*).

But I go to a very clean office and my teeth are professionally maintained. Because of this, I'll probably have my teeth my whole life. My dentist goes out of his way to keep pain to a minimum. From this perspective, which is just as valid as my automatic interpretation, I am *lucky* — I *get* to go to the dentist.

When I thought about it that way, my mood shifted. I felt better. I felt *fortunate* to live in a time when people can take care of their teeth. I felt lucky to live in a place where we have dentists.

That's how reframing works. It is surprisingly easy to do. All you have to do is:

1) Notice some circumstance is bringing you down.

2) Ask yourself if there is some other way to look at it.

There are several ways to create a reframe, but this one works very simply and directly. Just ask, "Is there another way to look at this?"

An alternative method for creating a reframe is to work backwards. First ask, "How would I *like* to feel about this?" And then ask yourself, "How would I have to see this in order to feel that way?"

So, for example, let's say Clark feels that he has too much to do and it stresses him out. So Clark asks, "How would I *like* to feel?" He thinks about it for a minute and comes up with this answer: "I want to feel relaxed. I still want to be motivated to get things done, but I want to feel at ease about what needs to be done."

Now, the question: How would Clark have to look at all his things to do in order to feel that way? Here are a few reframes Clark might come up with:

1) The huge abundance of things to do makes it easier to do *high-quality* things. Since I think up things to do faster than I could ever do them, I have to be selective. So it's like the process of brainstorming: You come up with lots of ideas, and then you discard some of them. And what you end up with is high quality.

2) This moment is like an hourglass. The moments can only occur *one at a time*. I can't push the sand through faster than it goes. I can take each task "one grain of sand at a time."

3) When I'm 95 years old and looking back on this time in my life, I would probably say, "Do a little less and enjoy a little more. Some day it will all be over."

Clark can keep coming up with ideas until he hits a reframe that really changes his feelings the way he wants. That's a very productive way to create reframes. Ask a question and come up with many answers.

Another thing that helps to come up with a reframe is to aim at a particular *kind* of reframe. So aim for a "learning experience" reframe, or a comparison reframe, for example.

Another way is to imagine your situation from different points of view. Imagine a younger person had the same situation and you tried to give her some perspective. How would you reframe it?

We'll explore a few more angles in the upcoming chapters, but the basic technique is to simply make a list of possible reframes.

And one other thing that helps you come up with good reframes: Before you sit down to make your list, do something that puts you in a good mood. Your good mood will boost your creativity.

Watching a funny movie, or even merely watching *twenty minutes* of a funny movie, measurably improves your ability to creatively come up with ideas. Exercise, listen to music, take a hot bath — do whatever you know will put you in a good mood (you can get ideas at Moodraiser.com). Then sit down and make your list.

And of course, you can do a brainstorming session with another person, or even *several* people.

But you don't *need* any of that. Although these ideas make it *easier* to come up with good reframes, they're not necessary. You can sit down right now and take a few minutes and create a good reframe. It is just a matter of taking the time to do it.

And even if you take the time and come up with a nice long list of possible reframes, it is possible that none of them are very good, but your time spent wasn't wasted. You have put that question solidly into your mind, and when you go on about your business, a part of your mind will still be working on it. Sometime afterward — a few hours, even a week later — something may happen or you'll hear something and you'll get a good reframe.

I remember once when I lived in an apartment building, I was bothered by noisy neighbors. They seemed to always have friends or family over and during the summer especially, because everyone's windows were open, all the noise would really bother me. I'm a writer. I always liked it quiet when I was writing.

It bothered me that it bothered me, if you know what I mean. And it didn't feel right to tell them to keep it down. It was, after all, in the middle of the day and they were just enjoying each other's company.

So I tried to reframe it, but my effort wasn't very successful. I came up with my list of possibilities, but none of them really did it for me. But obviously my mind was still working on it later when I came across a study that tested the creativity of three randomly-selected groups. All three groups were given creativity tests. One group was in a quiet room, another group was in a room with a moderate level of restaurant noises, and the third group was in a room with relatively loud traffic noise.

The group with the moderate level of noise came up with the most original ideas.

When I read that, the reframe I was seeking popped into my head! My neighbors were helping me to be original and creative. Ever since then, whenever they were noisy while I was writing, the sounds they made no longer bothered me. I thought they might be actually helping my writing. This kind of spontaneous reframe has happened to me many times, but only after I really tried.

So *put in the time* trying to think up reframes, even if you don't seem to be successful at first. Your effort plants that question deep in your mind, helping you recognize the perfect reframe when it pops into your head.

Another reframe I used at the time was to imagine that whoever was making noise was a friend of mine. I remember coming up with this because once one of my neighbors who I knew and liked was having a party one night and it didn't bother me at all.

I figured it must be because I liked that neighbor. Quite a few times when I heard noises from other apartments, I imagined my best friend lived there, and that his family was making the noise.

It totally shifted how I felt about the noise. I wouldn't be bothered at all by it, partly because I would know he wasn't being "inconsiderate" to me.

That means part of what made me upset must have been an assumption that those noisy neighbors were aware that their noise bothered me but they did it anyway, which wasn't likely since I'd never said anything to them about it.

In these and many other ways, I played with different perspectives and learned how much of a difference they could make. And in the process, I learned some practical methods for creating reframes.

DISARMING HOSTILITY

"If we could read the secret history of our enemies," wrote Henry Wadsworth Longfellow, "we should find in each man's life sorrow and suffering enough to disarm all hostility." I have just come across two good examples of this. The first was from Stephen Covey. He was riding a New York subway one morning. It was a peaceful ride with people reading the newspaper or looking out the window or resting with their eyes closed.

Then a man and his children got on. "The children were so loud and rambunctious," says Covey, "that instantly the whole climate changed." As it turns out, the man sat down right next to Covey and closed his eyes while the kids went wild. They were yelling and throwing things. Covey was irritated. How could this man ignore his children and their obnoxious behavior? Why didn't he do anything about it? Covey says, "It was easy to see that everyone else on the subway felt irritated, too."

Covey did the best he could to restrain his irritation and said, "Sir, your children are really disturbing a lot of people. I wonder if you couldn't control them a little more?"

The man replied, "Oh, you're right. I guess I should do something about it. We just came from the hospital where their mother died about an hour ago. I don't know what to think, and I guess they don't know how to handle it either."

As you can guess, this shifted Covey's perspective entirely and he instantly went from irritated to sympathetic.

The second example is from the book, *Team of Rivals*, a book about Abraham Lincoln's presidential cabinet.

Before Lincoln ran for president, he was a small-time attorney. But one day he was invited to participate in an important trial. He was to be co-counsel for the prosecution with a distinguished attorney named George Harding.

Harding wanted Lincoln because the judge deciding the case was familiar with Lincoln and liked him.

After Harding hired Lincoln, the case was moved to another city (with a different judge) so Harding hired a *different* co-counsel, Edwin Stanton. Lincoln didn't know about this change and kept working on the case because this was a big opportunity, or so he thought. But Harding and Stanton ignored and shunned Lincoln, at one point referring to Lincoln as a long-armed ape.

Stanton did not want Lincoln involved in the case, and Stanton made this painfully clear. Stanton avoided him at mealtimes, letting Lincoln eat alone even though the two attorneys ate and stayed at the same hotel. Stanton never asked Lincoln to even *show* him the considerable amount of work Lincoln had already done on the case.

As I was reading this, I thought Stanton was clearly a rude, mean person. Stanton insulted and humiliated Lincoln. A little later in the book, I learned more about Stanton, and he had enough sorrow and suffering in his life to disarm all my hostility.

Stanton had been married and was deeply in love. He was happier than he'd ever been in his life. He and his wife had two children together. Everything was wonderful, but then one tragedy after another tore his world apart.

First their daughter died of scarlet fever. While he was still reeling from that heartbreak, Stanton's wife died of bilious fever.

Stanton almost went insane with grief. Stanton's sister came to live with him, and she said he often wandered through the house at night sobbing, and screaming, "Where is Mary!?"

A little while later, Stanton's younger brother got a fever than damaged his brain. He was "unhinged" and purposefully cut his own neck with a sharp instrument and bled to death, spraying blood all over the room, even up to the ceiling. Stanton lived nearby and had to come take care of things. His brother had a wife and three kids that Stanton was now responsible for.

His brother's gruesome suicide was Stanton's last straw. Before these tragedies, Stanton was a cheerful man, full of goodwill toward others. From that point on, and for the rest of his life, Stanton was glum and grumpy. And sometimes rude.

I imagined myself losing my son, losing my wife, losing my brother, and in so doing, I didn't resent Stanton for his rudeness to Lincoln. I felt sorry for him. Nobody should have to endure that kind of anguish. I believe that's what Longfellow was talking about.

There is only one problem with Longfellow's very sensible outlook — we don't very often find out the secret history of our enemies. Maybe the point is to give people the benefit of the doubt. If someone treats you poorly, you can reasonably *assume* they have sorrow and suffering enough to disarm your hostility, and you'll probably be right. And even if you're not, you have saved yourself a little suffering. It is less painful to feel sympathy than to feel anger.

I would like to add one caveat to this practical advice: Some people may be more than rude. Some people may actually harm you or deplete your resources or try to take advantage of your good nature. They are a special case.

But for the normal, relatively harmless (but grumpy) people you come across in the course of your travels, it will probably save you unnecessary suffering if you make Longfellow's assumption.

The important principle is to never settle for a perspective that makes you feel bad unnecessarily or impedes your ability to successfully deal with a situation. Explore different perspectives. Your perspective makes a big difference in how you feel and in what you do. It would be foolish to let your mind haphazardly create perspectives and then feel stuck with them when *you have the power* to create better ones.

Take the time and play with your own perspectives. One place to start is the method in the next chapter.

ONE GOOD REFRAMING PROCESS

On Amazon.com, there are 29 reviews of my first book. Most of them are positive, but three of them are negative, at least to some degree. And of course, because of the human brain's negative bias, the negative ones stick out in my mind and have more emotional impact than all the other positive reviews combined.

I've been using three reframes for this and they work so well I'm not bothered by the negative reviews. In fact, I'm actually *glad* they are there. I'm not kidding.

There is a difference between "trying to think positive" or "putting a positive spin" on something and actually reframing it. You can tell if you have a genuine reframe if your feelings change. I really, honestly do not feel any negative feelings from these critical reviews. If I still did, then I would know I'm just trying to talk myself into something I really don't believe. Here are my three reframes:

1. I get to find out what some people don't like about my book, and since I plan on writing more books, it might be useful information.

2. A few bad reviews will help people make *a better decision* about buying my book, which should in theory prevent people who wouldn't like it from buying it, thus improving my reviews over time, and saving people the trouble of getting something they don't want.

3. The few bad reviews keep a buyer's expectations from soaring too high. If a potential customer only read the positive reviews, she might think *Self-Help Stuff That Works* is the answer to all the world's problems, which it isn't. Not only that, but the bad reviews all criticize the same thing, and it is one of the things that the positive reviews almost all praise: That the chapters are short. The people who criticized it wanted more detail. The ones who praised it *liked* the fact that the chapters are brief,

to the point, and practical. By having both reviews on there, a potential book buyer can make a better, more informed decision.

In other words, about the bad reviews, I can genuinely say: "That's good!"

I created these reframes deliberately. When I first read those reviews, I felt bad. It was a little upsetting. My feelings were a bit hurt.

So I sat down and wrote as many reframes as I could in a half hour. I set a timer and made myself continue to come up with reframes until the timer went off.

Then I looked through them. Most of them were not very good and some of them were down-right stupid, but the three above made sense to me and changed the way I felt about the reviews.

That's a good method for creating a reframe. Make a long list. In your effort to come up with reframes, you'll come up with good ones and bad ones, but some of the bad ones will give you ideas that'll help you come up with good ones. How's that for a reframe of the dumb ideas?

Set a target — either a number or a set amount of time, and set the target before you start. "I will come up with twenty reframes" or "I will keep coming up with reframes for fifteen minutes."

The more important the issue is, the more time you are justified to put into it. The more time you put into it (or the higher your target number) the more likely you are to come up with a really great reframe.

Don't judge your reframes until you're done coming up with them. Just keep going. When the time is up, or when you've hit your number, *then* look through them and see if any seem like sensible ways to look at the situation.

Circle the ones that make sense to you or strike a nerve, or write them on a separate piece of paper and post them somewhere. Let the new ways of thinking sink in and see if they make a difference.

When you find a good reframe, something that made you angry or afraid or hurt could actually turn into something you're glad about.

REFRAMING A
DISADVANTAGE

William Coleman had only fifty percent of normal vision in one eye and only twenty-five percent in the other. The year was 1899 and although the electric light bulb had already been invented, not many people had one because electricity wasn't available in many places.

Even with electricity, the light bulbs in those days weren't very bright. As a law student, the only way William could study at night was to have his parents read his texts to him.

His poor eyesight was obviously a disadvantage. Or was it?

One night William walked into a store brightly lit by a pressurized gas lamp. It was producing more illumination than he'd ever seen — it was bright enough to read by! He said it was the most important moment of his life.

Without the "disadvantage" of poor eyesight, it might not have meant much to him. But since it *did* mean so much, he got involved in a gas lamp business — so involved he eventually *owned* the company.

A hundred years later, the Coleman Company is still in business with sales at about half a billion dollars a year. And even though electric light illuminates most of the world, people still use Coleman Lanterns when they go camping. More than a million of those original pressurized gas lanterns are sold every year.

If there's something you think is a disadvantage, think again. *Assume* there will be an advantage in it and then find it or make it. This intention is a fundamental key to a good attitude. With it, the inevitable setbacks in life won't bring you down as much and you will handle problems more effectively.

To assume you will find an advantage is a reframe. It is similar to the old adage that "trouble brings the seeds of good fortune."

I know some people would scoff at this reframe. It might remind them of some annoyingly positive people to whom "everything is great," but somehow, behind their forced smile, you can see it's all a façade, and it just kind of wears you out to be with them. But this idea can be used with depth and efficacy, not merely as a way to show a pleasant face to the world or to hide your pain from yourself. It can be done with intelligence and wisdom. It can make you more capable of solving real problems and confronting your challenges with courage.

Many people think that *cynicism* and *pessimism* show they are mature. They think only the foolish and naïve would be optimistic.

Somehow cynicism is *cool*. But it is actually dangerous and unhealthy. It makes you feel bad unnecessarily. It makes you less capable and less successful. And the bad attitude it creates is contagious.

Reframing is *practical* and healthy. Taking control of the way you look at things, and deliberately creating reframes that serve you is one of the smartest things you can do.

GOOD CAME OUT OF IT

In a study at Washington University in St. Louis, researchers interviewed people who had experienced either a plane crash, a tornado, or a mass shooting.

They interviewed the survivors a few weeks after the traumatic event and then again three years later.

In the first interview, some people said they could find something good that came out of the event. Some reported that they realized life was too short not to pursue their most important goals, or they realized how important their family was to them. Three years later, *those* were the people who recovered from the trauma most successfully.

Now, a plane crash, a tornado or a mass shooting is not wonderful in *anybody's* book. The most natural way to look at these things is as disasters and tragedies. But if you've been through something like that, you have a choice about how you look at it. And the frame, the point of view you adopt, has consequences.

In the research on post-traumatic stress disorder, you'll find references to something called "post-traumatic benefits." Professor of psychiatry Frank Ochberg says some people who have been captives in a hostage situation think the experience made them wiser. Ochberg says, "They say, 'I'm going to shift my priorities. I'm going to spend more time with people I love.'"

In his book, *Hostage*, James Campbell wrote, "I've talked with hostages who have declared that the experience was in some ways beneficial. After this, they'll say, 'It got me rethinking things. Life is finite; let's not waste it. Am I living the way I should be?'"

In an interview in *Psychology Today*, the late Carl Sagan said, "This is my third time having to deal with intimations of mortality. And every time it's a character-building experience. You get a much clearer perspective on what's important and what isn't, the preciousness and beauty of life...I would recommend almost dying to everybody. I think it's a really good experience."

Think now about something you normally consider a disadvantage. Are you in debt? Did you have a rough childhood? Were you poor? Didn't have the advantages wealthier kids had? Do you lack education? Do you have a bad habit or a personal quirk? Has something terrible happened to you?

What's *good* about it? Or how could you *capitalize* on your "disadvantage?" If you don't get a good answer right away, that only means it's a tough question. Try *living in that question* for several weeks or months. Ponder it while you drive. Wonder about it while you shower. Ask yourself the question while you eat lunch. Live with the question and you will get answers.

General Grant, the man credited with winning the Civil War, had a strange quirk his whole life. He never retraced his steps. He couldn't do it. So if he was riding his horse and took a wrong fork in the road, he could not bring himself to turn back. He frequently commented on this peculiar "glitch" of his.

But then along came the Civil War. For a long time after the war broke out, there was a lot of bloodshed and violence, but no *progress*. Tens of thousands of soldiers were dying but it was a stalemate. Union generals would advance and retreat, advance and retreat. Nothing was being gained and massive numbers of young men were being killed on both sides.

Then Grant captured a critical fort. Grant's quirk caused him to never turn back. So when he began to attack a fort, he couldn't stop until the fort was taken.

Grant's capture of the fort was one of the few real victories thus far in the war. So he was promoted. And he began defeating and capturing and advancing, and he kept getting promoted until he was the head of the whole Union army. His strange little quirk was partly responsible for his success. Because of his war record, he was voted into two terms as President of the United States.

Grant took advantage of his quirk. He made his disadvantage one of his greatest strengths, and you should do the same. Take advantage of what you are, where you are, and when you are. It's the only practical way to deal with "disadvantages."

If you have a tendency to simply feel bad about your disadvantages, even *that* can become an advantage. Overcoming that tendency might teach you something valuable — something you couldn't have learned without it. And you can teach what you learned to your child, making a huge difference to the whole trajectory of her or his life.

Trying to make the best of something helps create solutions. It makes things better. It is even better for your health. It keeps you from feeling as bad when bad stuff happens, and that's important because negative emotions are not good for your health. As Richard H. Hoffmann, MD, said:

"The human body is a delicately adjusted mechanism. Whenever its even tenor is startled by some intruding emotion like sudden fright, anger or worry, the sympathetic nervous system flashes an emergency signal and the organs and glands spring into action. The adrenal glands shoot into the blood stream a surcharge of adrenaline which raises the blood sugar above normal needs. The pancreas then secretes insulin to burn the excess fuel. But this bonfire burns not only the excess but the normal supply. The result is a blood sugar shortage and an underfeeding of the vital organs. So the adrenals supply another charge, the pancreas burns the fuel again, and the vicious cycle goes on. This battle of the glands brings on exhaustion."

Bad feelings play havoc on your system. The all-purpose reframe that "trouble brings seeds of good fortune" allows you to consider the possibility that a bad event or disadvantage might not be as bad as it seems at the moment, and in a sense, the reframe makes it possible to *procrastinate* feeling bad.

Procrastinate long enough, and you might just skip it altogether. And it could give you enough time to actually find or create an advantage from the "misfortune." In the meantime, you'll be happier and healthier.

Volunteers at the *Common Cold Research Unit* in Britain filled out a questionnaire, and then were exposed to the common cold virus. The researcher, Sheldon Cohen, discovered that the more *positive* the volunteers' attitudes were, the *less* likely they would catch a cold. And even when they did catch a cold, the more positive their attitude was, the more mild their symptoms were.

Take the time to reframe your misfortunes and disadvantages. Make the best of them. It is good for your mood, your health, and your future.

HOW TO GAIN PERSPECTIVE

The late Viktor Frankl, the psychiatrist and survivor of Hitler's concentration camps you read about in Chapter 5, often helped his patients gain perspective, and when he successfully did this, it changed their lives.

For example, Frankl helped an elderly and severely depressed man who came to him for therapy. The man's wife had died and she had meant more to him than anything in the world.

How could Frankl help this man gain some perspective on such a tragic event? "What would have happened," Frankl asked the man, "if you had died first, and your wife would have survived you?"

The man answered: "Oh, for her this would have been terrible; how she would have suffered!"

"You see," said Frankl, "such a suffering has been spared her, and it is *you* who have spared her this suffering; but now, you have to pay for it by surviving and mourning her."

The man didn't say anything. He shook Dr. Frankl's hand and calmly left. He'd gained an entirely different perspective on his situation in an instant.

Frankl wrote, "Suffering ceases to be suffering in some way at the moment it finds a meaning, such as the meaning of a sacrifice."

Frankl changed the man's perspective, and it had a profound affect on the man's feelings. When you know how to gain perspective, you know how to change the meaning of a circumstance. Your new perspective changes the meaning of the event, which changes the feelings you have in response, which changes what actions you take. And it all changes in an instant.

WHAT WOULD HELP?

Here's how to gain perspective in the simplest and most direct way: When something happens, ask yourself, "What perspective would help right now?"

Klassy is on a twelve-day trip as I write this. I couldn't go. During the planning stage, I was sad about this. I miss her when she's gone. But I asked myself, "What perspective would help right now?"

I realized I would be alone and entirely un-interrupted by any consideration of another person, and this is, of course, potentially useful for a writer, and I thought I should take full advantage of it.

The question shifted my attention in a new direction, changing my feelings about the upcoming event.

Ask yourself the question. That's how to gain perspective quickly and easily. Klassy has been gone four days now and I've been doing some great writing. I'm able to concentrate more than usual. All this attention to my work has also kept my mind from dwelling on how much I miss her.

When you're facing an upcoming event you really don't want to happen, try asking yourself, "What perspective would help right now?" If no answer comes immediately to mind, *that's not the end of it*. Ask the question over and over. Or sit down and write out a list of ten answers to the question.

The question works for events that *will* happen, and it also works for events that have *already* happened. For example, right after I self-published my first book, I called bookstores to ask if I could fax them a blurb on my new book, and about a third of the people I called had a negative reaction. They were probably bombarded by ads, which wasted their fax machine's paper (this was before fax machines could receive a fax without printing it), and besides, I may have interrupted the person with my phone call.

For whatever reason, I got some negative reactions, and when I did, it brought me down. When I got several negative reactions in a row, I felt dejected and I thought negative things like, "This is hopeless."

But I asked myself, "What perspective would help right now?" Almost immediately I thought, "The world *needs* this book!" The negativity I heard on the other end of the phone line didn't make these people happy or healthy or more successful. They needed help! And not just them, but lots of people would be helped by my book. I couldn't give up now.

With this new perspective, I shifted from dejected to *determined and motivated* — a nice shift. I went back at it with renewed resolve.

The three reframe techniques I like the most are comparison reframes, which you read about earlier, visualizing goals, which you will read about shortly, and gratitude.

Comparison reframes take advantage of the fact that your mind naturally and automatically compares your situation to something else. Usually to something better, so it makes you feel bad.

But you can, of course, deliberately compare your situation to something worse, and feel better.

Having a goal almost automatically reframes many of the setbacks in your life. It casts the setback in a new light. For example, Nelson Mandela had been in prison for much of his life. He was fighting for the end of apartheid in South Africa and the government had locked him up. He still had his goal, though.

One day they moved him to a new area of the prison, away from the people he knew. He was now isolated. He was in a dark, damp cell instead of the sunnier cell he used to have. All of this made him feel bad at first.

But then he started thinking this might be a good time to begin negotiations with the government — away from the eyes of his fellow political prisoners (many of whom would have tried to dissuade him from negotiating). Because of his goal, he had a different perspective on his new cell. In a sense, focusing on his goal changed his perspective about his circumstances.

PLAYING WITH PERSPECTIVES

Today I went for a jog. I went along the lake, the same way I usually go, and I noticed I was looking at it with this perspective: "I've seen this same scenery hundreds of times." But then I thought about the fact that some day this won't be here any more or I won't be here any more. Some day this moment, these times, these days will be gone. And I'll probably look back fondly on these times and wish I could see this scenery again, and this age again, and these *times* again. But I won't be able to. This time will pass and I'll never be able to go back except in my memory.

This thought changed my perspective, and it changed the way I felt. I didn't have to go out of my way to do this. I was already running. I was already thinking. I didn't have to stop doing what I was doing. I just changed the way I was thinking a little bit, and it changed the quality of my experience for the better.

"I've already seen this scenery hundreds of times" is one perspective — one of many possible perspectives, and not the most life-giving by any means.

"Some day I'll look back on this fondly," is another perspective, and one with more value. It has more value in the sense that it helps me *be here* and savor this moment. It makes me feel better.

When I thought about looking back on the scenery fondly, I remembered doing that before — thinking back to some moment in my childhood or even a few years ago, and feeling a longing for being there and experiencing it again. And then I said to myself, gently, "And some day you'll think of this moment right now in the same way." The end result was somehow I generated a feeling of longing *for what I was experiencing at that moment*, and it was a beautiful experience.

By playing with my perspective, I transformed a routine experience into something memorable and meaningful.

Sometimes when Klassy and I are taking a walk through our fair city, we imagine we are tourists, looking at the city for the first time, and again, it changes our perspective.

Sometimes we look at each other, pretending we have just met, and this also gives us a different perspective, allowing a greater appreciation for each other.

These are all ways to trick the mind into being here and experiencing the world rather than taking things for granted.

GRATITUDE AS A REFRAME

While a different perspective can often make you feel gratitude, you can use gratitude itself to gain a new perspective. And this simple act can make you measurably happier. In the study where subjects spent only five minutes a day writing in a journal, answering the question, "What am I grateful for?"

people became happier. Even *after they stopped doing it*, they were still measurably happier for some time after.

Gratitude is itself a reframe. And it can significantly change your state. Back before we'd read about the gratitude studies, Klassy casually gave me a very simple suggestion that made me happier. She said, "Whenever you feel discouraged, think of something you're grateful for."

I've done it hundreds, maybe thousands of times now, and every time it is surprisingly easy to think of something I'm grateful for, and it makes me feel better every time.

Does gratitude sound like work? Does it seem like "counting your blessings" would be a kind of chore? That's the wrong way to think about it. You never need to feel like you *should* sit down and write in a journal for a specified length of time, or try to write down a specified number of "things I feel grateful for." That's how they do it in the experiments, but of course that's because it's an *experiment*. They have to test quantifiable, measurable tasks in an experiment. That doesn't mean *you* have to.

Generating a little gratitude works well on the fly and in your head just as well as it does writing it down in a journal. It's not a chore at all — just a simple question to ask yourself. It only takes a few moments (just long enough to think of something).

And as soon as you think of something, you'll feel noticeably better.

I've found that if the first thing I think of doesn't raise my mood enough, I can easily ask myself what *else* I'm grateful for.

You and I naturally have our attention on our goals and what we'd like to attain in the future, and the mind naturally compares our goals to what we have now. It compares what we have with what we *want* to have. That's motivating sometimes, but it can also make you feel dissatisfied.

It is equally legitimate — and ought to get equal billing — to think about what you *have* (compared to others or compared to your past), or what you have *gained*, or what you are just plain glad about.

Try it the next time you feel discouraged or frustrated. Ask yourself, "What one thing am I grateful for?" And see what happens. It's a simple, all-purpose mood raiser you can keep in your back pocket and use a lot.

When you do, you'll be happier.

Use comparison reframes, gratitude, and your own goals to gain a new perspective on an upcoming event, on the past, or on a situation you're dealing with right in the present.

Or you can simply ask, "What perspective would help right now?" And start coming up with answers. A mastery of perspective can reliably, authentically, and measurably change your life.

A LESSON IN REFRAMING FROM GROUNDHOG DAY

In the movie, *Groundhog Day*, Bill Murray plays a weatherman named Phil. Self-centered, bitter, and sarcastic, Phil is not a happy man and he tends to make other peoples' lives more difficult. One day Phil has to go to a little town to cover a Groundhog Day festival, and the next day he wakes up and it is still Groundhog Day. The next day the same thing happens. He has to live the same day, Groundhog Day, again and again. Every morning he wakes up, he's in the same place on the same day. For weeks, months, *years*.

Phil feels trapped, and in his anger, his first reaction is to try to take selfish advantage of the situation. He steals money, drives recklessly, and tricks women into having sex with him. Even when he gets locked up in jail, the next morning he wakes up back in his bed and nobody knows anything about what happened the day before. It's like it never happened to anyone but him. So he can do whatever he wants without suffering any consequences. So he does. But this doesn't make him happy.

All the while, Phil talks to Rita, his producer, every day. It slowly dawns on him that he loves her. Of course, she only knows him as the ego-centric jerk he has been so far, so he is frustrated. He sees her and talks to her every day, but from her point of view, up until yesterday he has proven himself to be a pretentious, conceited narcissist.

At first he tries to be phony, learning all about Rita's likes and dislikes, and trying to get her to fall for him. But no matter how far he gets the night before, every morning she thinks he's a jerk again.

Finally he gives up, gets depressed, and decides the only way out of this nightmare is to kill himself. He drives his truck off a cliff, jumps off a building, gets in a bath and drops a plugged-in toaster in the water, etc. But every morning he wakes up in bed again, not a scratch on him.

Finally he gives up and starts being his honest self. And when he does, Rita responds to it. One day he hangs out with her all day and he tells her what's going on. He's stuck in Groundhog Day and there's nothing he can do about it.

But she responds with something that reframes his situation for him. She says, "Sometimes I *wish* I had a thousand lifetimes."

All of us watching have felt some sympathy for Phil. What a terrible torture to be stuck reliving the same day over and over and over. But Rita was right. Haven't we all wished we had more time? Aren't there things you would do if you had an unlimited amount of time? Things you would learn? Things you would try to experience?

Her reframe changes his attitude completely. He decides to bloom where he is planted. He decides to accept his situation and make the best of it. He decides to fulfill himself and be happy. And he does.

He learns to do ice sculpting and to play the piano — things that take time, things he'd always wanted to do but never had the time because he was too busy trying to win fame and fortune. Now he has all the time he would ever need. And Phil starts finding people in need and helping them just because he likes doing it.

He becomes a happy, fulfilled, satisfied man.

And then, of course, Rita falls in love with him, and he wakes up and it is finally the day after Groundhog Day.

The movie is a good demonstration of how dramatically life can change with a new perspective. All his objective circumstances were the same as they were when he was trying to kill himself.

When he saw his situation as a trap, as a sentence, he was miserable. But when he saw the *opportunity* in the circumstances, when he chose to make the best of things as they were, he transformed. And he was happier. Everyone he came into contact with was happier too.

How can this apply to you? Watch the movie and think about what you have in your life that you think of as a trap. What unchanging circumstance do you have that you resist or hate?

Now ask yourself, "What might be *good* about this? How might I take advantage of this? How could I thrive and fulfill myself right where I am?"

Honestly pondering those questions can help generate a reframe that shifts your attitude, improves your mood, and opens the possibility of surprising new opportunities for joy.

REFRAME
BY VISUALIZING GOALS

If you listen carefully to what successful people say about accomplishing goals, you'll find a consistent common thread: They envision their goals in detail. If you're like me, you've heard this many times in interviews or read it in biographies, and completely ignored it.

I ignored it because I am "not a visual person." I didn't think I was very good at visualizing. But visualization is a *learnable* skill. You get better with practice.

I can't believe what a difference this simple practice has made. It sometimes seems like magic. I try to stay skeptical and explain things using verifiable evidence. I know how easy it is to come to false conclusions, so I've explained the stunning results to myself by noting that when I envision my goals clearly, it focuses my mind and increases my motivation, which it certainly does.

It also produces a reverse engineering effect. That is, when I envision my goals clearly, I automatically start thinking about "how it happened." And that gets me to thinking about what I'm doing now.

For example, one of my goals is a million subscribers for my blog, Moodraiser.com. As I imagined looking at my Feedburner stats (statistics for my subscribers) and seeing a million subscribers, I thought about some possible ways this could happen. I wasn't *trying* to think this way; it just happens naturally when visualizing a goal.

One of the things I thought of is the possibility that someone famous would mention it on their television show, causing a huge number of new visitors, many of whom would really like the blog and subscribe to it. And then they'd share the articles with their friends, causing even *more* people to subscribe, etc.

But then it occurred to me if it gets mentioned on a popular television show, and all these new people were going to look at the blog, *it better be really good*. I realized it would be embarrassing if all these people showed up on a day when the front page article was only so-so. Up to that time I was kind of casual about what I posted because I only had 400 subscribers.

See what happened? By simply envisioning the goal, I automatically started thinking backwards — back in time to the present — and it altered what I was doing in the present in such a way that *the goal was more likely to happen.* This kind of thinking comes about without trying. All you need to do is visualize your goal. The reverse engineering effect happens all by itself.

Another practical result of clearly visualizing a goal is the production of great ideas. Somehow the process of visualizing your goal stimulates your creativity. Surprising new ideas will start popping into your head spontaneously.

Because you have such a clear picture of your future, you will see your present differently. When you regularly envision your goals, you will find that you quite naturally reframe "negative events." You start seeing setbacks more as useful information and less as a cause for demoralization.

These are some of the *explainable* results of envisioning goals. Something else happens too. It seems almost supernatural. Maybe at least part of it is the involvement of your reticular activator, which is a part of the brain the stays on alert. Its job is to make you notice some things and ignore other things (if you noticed everything, you'd be too distracted to function). When you buy a new

Prius, it seems like the whole world has recently bought them too, because *you notice them everywhere.* That's the reticular activator at work.

But however we explain it, envisioning goals produces a whole host of positive effects. Give it a shot and see what I mean.

HOW TO ENVISION GOALS

Visualizing a goal is a pretty straightforward task. But here are a few tips to make it more effective:

1. Relax first. Use any method, as long as it makes you deeply relaxed without putting you to sleep. It's important to be relaxed. When you try to visualize your goal without relaxing first, negative or anxious thoughts are more likely to worm their way into your visualizations.

2. First remember a success. It helps to remember a goal you've successfully achieved in the past. And then, in the same sitting, imagine your new goal.

Remembering past successes will emotionally enhance your visualizations of the future, and can greatly strengthen your confidence in your ability to achieve your goals.

3. See your goal in detail. The first thing to envision is the moment you realize you have achieved your goal. If you have a goal of publishing your book, you'll know it's published when you're holding the printed copy of your book in your hands for the first time.

It will be sent to you by mail. So envision getting the package in the mail, and with trembling fingers opening it with your spouse, pulling out the book, and looking at it.

Envision it in every sensory detail. Where are you? What does the book smell like? What time of day is it? What expression do you see on your spouse's face? How do you feel?

Every time you relax and envision your goal, try to see new details you haven't imagined before. Make it as real and vivid as possible.

And allow yourself to imagine *past* that point. What will you do next? What will happen afterward? Imagine the consequences of your achievement a week later, a month later, a year later.

4. Sit up. Don't lie down. When you lie down, your images tend to drift more randomly and you're more likely to fall asleep. Sitting up gives you better control of your images.

5. Do it several times a week. Spend some time on it. Ten to twenty minutes at a time is good.

6. Don't force positivity. If something negative appears in your visualizations and keeps popping up, consider it a message from your unconscious mind or the mute right hemisphere of your brain, or your inner wisdom.

Consider it a message, and seek to discover the lesson. What is it telling you that will help you achieve the goal? And then visualize yourself resolving that problem and successfully accomplishing your purpose.

If you have big goals and you work hard, but your goal has seemed frustratingly elusive up until now, you might have been missing this one vital ingredient: Clearly envisioning your goal.

Give it a try. In addition to all its other positive effects, clearly visualizing your goal will help you reframe setbacks.

WHAT MYTH DO YOU LIVE BY?

O n his first military campaign, George Washington made a terrible mistake. The American colonies had not yet rebelled — that was still twenty years down the road.

Washington was working for Britain at the time, which was in a "cold war" with France. The two countries were tussling with each other for territory all over the world, including the area near Virginia.

One day Washington and his troops spotted a party of French camping in their territory, and attacked them, killing ten men and capturing the rest.

He shot first and asked questions later. He found out it was a *diplomatic* party, and one of the men he killed was an important French ambassador. Washington had made a huge mistake. The two major military powers of that time ended their cold war and entered a hot war.

Imagine, for the moment, that you were Washington, and you made that mistake. What would you tell yourself about it? How would the mistake fit into the overall pattern of your life?

In other words: What kind of *story* do you live in? Where do you think you come from and where do you think you're going?

You live by a story. Have you ever thought of it that way? Each of us has a story, and we are the main character in that story. If I interviewed you for a couple of weeks, I could probably piece together a coherent story that you live by even if you've never really thought about it yourself. It's your life story and it contains within it the meaning of your life.

For example, one story Washington could have told himself was: "I am destined for failure." His father died young, his mother was a nag. Compared to his contemporaries, he was poor. Killing the French ambassador could have been the final straw. He might have concluded that he wasn't cut out for military work and given up, climbed inside a bottle and we would never have heard of him.

That's one possible story. That's one context within which he could have lived his life. And do you see that the story leads to certain feelings and certain actions consistent with the story?

Your story is the big frame of your life. It is the overarching view you have of your life.

Here's another possible frame: Washington *could* have believed he was destined to make his mark in the world, and that his mistake was the most important lesson he was ever to learn. "Divine Providence," he could have told himself, "is preparing me for a great task. I must learn all I can from this mistake for it may affect the future of the world."

Do you think he would feel differently about the circumstances of his life with this story? Of course he would. Same circumstances, different story. But the heroic story would make him learn important military lessons from his mistake and it would help him persist and endure hardships that would overwhelm or devastate a weaker person. The story would give him strength.

Judging by the letters he wrote home, the story he lived by was a lot more like the second one than the first one. And because he lived by that more inspiring story — because he viewed his life from that point of view — he persisted and he learned and he *did* make a difference.

Man of La Mancha, a musical made in 1972, is based on the story, *Don Quixote*, by Miguel de Cervantes. It's an entertaining story, but it's also profound.

Don Quixote sees the world as a "quest," as an adventure, and he sees a poor kitchen maid as a lady of unsurpassed beauty and chastity. He dreams the impossible dream, he fights the unbeatable foe, he looks at life as a challenge to do good in the face of evil and make the world a better place. He wants to dedicate his victories to the kitchen maid, his Lady.

She is bitter about life, full of anger. "Why do you do these things?" she asks him.

"What things?" he asks.

She bursts out in frustration, "It's *ridiculous*, the things you do!"

He answers simply, "I come in a world of iron to make a world of gold."

"The world's a dung heap," she says, "and we are maggots that crawl on it."

These are two very different stories by two people who are standing in the same objective reality. Yet one lives a life of nobility and beauty and adventure, and the other lives in filth and misery and hatred.

What kind of story do *you* live? Is it heroic? Or is it bland? Do you have a sense of destiny? Or do you have a sense of emptiness? What do you think is your destiny? The destiny of Earth? The destiny of the human race?

The story you tell yourself — the myth within which you live your life — strongly affects your feelings and the ultimate outcome of your life.

And it can change. You can change it deliberately.

THE MYTHS WE LIVE BY

Myths have been part of humankind since very near the beginning. We call them myths when they are other people's stories; we call them true when the story is our own.

A shaman sitting around the campfire twenty thousand years ago telling his people how their tribe came to be wasn't sharing what he thought of as a "myth" or fun little story; the story he told was the context of their daily lives. It was the pattern each of their experiences fit into. It was their "frame." It gave their lives *meaning*. It gave each of them a purpose for their existence. It enriched their lives...or it deadened it, depending on the story.

Some of the stories we hear from pre-scientific people seem quaint — even ridiculous — to us; we all now know that the earth is not sitting on the back of a giant turtle; we know the universe wasn't created by the wind.

If those pre-scientific people took a ride in a space shuttle and looked at the earth, they could see for themselves there's no giant turtle. And they would come up with a different story. *But they would come up with a story.* Everyone has either accepted a story from their culture or their family, or created one of their own. Everyone has a story they live. Including you.

It's important to live within a story that gives your life dignity and purpose. It'll make a difference in your life. And you don't have to force yourself to believe in an old myth if you don't believe it. Your "myth," to enrich your life, has to fit into your existing knowledge. It has to be true for you.

Because we know so much about the world, many of the old myths are difficult to believe in. Our security-blankets have been snatched away. And for many people, the modern stories they live by are empty, desolate, negative and hopeless. But it doesn't have to be that way.

We now know the universe is inconceivably vast. We know the earth is not the center of everything. We know the size of stars and galaxies are beyond our ability to grasp, and they dwarf us and our lives in comparison. But that knowledge doesn't mean you have to live by a desolate story. It lends itself to nobility and heroism just as easily.

For example, you also know that this one little planet is the only one we know of with life on it. Life is precious. The fact that you and I exist at all is utterly amazing! The existence of the universe, and the existence of life is nothing short of awe-inspiring.

Many people take this scientific knowledge and — without any leaps of faith — create for themselves a story with meaning. For example, they may decide it is their sacred duty to protect and preserve this planet and its precious forms of life.

A person in a position of power may work for policies to prevent animals from becoming extinct or policies to clean up pollution or policies to promote cooperation with other nations.

A mother may devote her life to her children and give them wisdom and courage and an appreciation for this rare planet and the miracle of life.

A secretary at an attorney's office may devote some of his spare time to writing letters to his representatives on issues he thinks are important, fighting the noble battle for Life.

Anybody in any position may play an important and even crucial part in the way things unfold in the future.

You may make an important difference.

You don't think so? Neither did George Washington in the first part of his life. And what if he hadn't helped lead the colonies in their fight for freedom? What if he was the crucial difference and we lost the war? What if our experiment with democracy and human rights had failed? It was not a "self-evident truth," it was an *invention*; it never existed in the long history of our species.

If the colonists' fight against the King of England had failed, would kings and fascist dictators rule the world today? Would the idea of individual human rights have disappeared?

Who can say what a difference he made? Who knows what difference *you* will make? Your life isn't over.

In the struggle for the right of women to vote in the United States, one obscure man made a difference. He was a representative in a small state. I don't even know his name. But the right of women to vote (which had won in the Senate by only *one* vote) had to win in the House. And it did — again *by one vote*, and that one vote was our hero: A representative in a small state who was expected to vote against it.

But his mother wrote him a letter and urged him to do the right thing. Her letter moved him, and he voted, and the world has never been the same.

His mother may not have done another significant thing in her life, but what she did made a difference to hundreds of millions of women and to the future of the United States and the world.

All those small acts of integrity she committed in her life that earned her son's respect led up to that one important moment when she changed his mind and changed the lives of millions forever after.

Each small, relatively meaningless act of her life — when cast in this new frame — had meaning and purpose. She may have realized that; maybe not. She may have lived a life couched in a story of nobility and heroism; or maybe she thought of herself as just one worthless person in a sea of worthless people.

We don't know what story she lived. But that isn't important now. She has passed on.

You, however, are alive and kicking. Your story is important.

You may be destined to make a difference. You may be the one person who turns the tide. Something important may depend on your goodness or your wisdom or your inner strength. And all the circumstances of your life right now, especially the parts you don't like, may be perfectly preparing you for the part you will play in the destiny of the earth.

Some people make a difference with their lives but don't know it, because what they did only set the stage for what came later, but what came later could only have happened if that stage was set.

Whether you see the results of your strength and goodness isn't the point. The point is that the story you live makes a difference in your life right now, regardless of what happens later.

If you have a cynical or empty or tragic story right now, it may make all the difference that you're reading this. This may be your turning point. And your belief that it is your mission to do what you can may be what keeps you trying against the odds, and it may be that *because* you try against the odds, you make a crucial difference.

Your story is to some degree a self-fulfilling prophecy. Make it a good one. Create a story that gives you dignity and purpose and meaning and strength of character. Teach that story to your children.

You may be the one.

LIVE!
DEATH APPROACHES

If you only had a very short time to live; if a credible medical authority said you would die very soon, you'd live differently because you knew you were dying. Death would be so close, you could not avoid its presence.

So what if you knew for a fact you had only weeks, not years, then only days, then only hours, then minutes, then gone forever? Life as you've known it would be completely and irrevocably gone.

If you knew, you'd live differently.

But *why* would you live differently? Because the way you live depends on your view of things and a death sentence would be an unequivocal, un-mitigated, *transcendent* reframe.

But the fact is, you don't know when you will die, and so you, like the rest of us, live as if you've got plenty of time. By not thinking about our own impending death, we get to avoid the horror, but we also miss out on something really good.

People who have been given a terminal diagnosis say that knowing we only have months before we die tends to wake us up out of our stupor. We are, in a sense, drugged by petty dramas, rendered semiconscious of our own life.

Almost every complaint we normally have seems petty compared to death. Car troubles, money troubles, arguments over the everyday ache of broken hearts, broken homes, broken dreams — we would *gladly* have them rather than death.

Pondering our own death makes us sit up and take notice of what's really and truly the most dear. And people who have faced death often say it was a gift to (as the song says) "live like you were dying." People who face death talk sweeter and give forgiveness they've been denying.

People who face death begin to really live, really care, really love. The bucket list of things you want to do before you die becomes doable. The closeness of death helps us find the time to claim them. We call old friends. We go hang gliding. We take the trip and watch the island sunset together. We finish important tasks. Write our great works. Paint what we see in our hearts.

We don't waste our remaining precious hours in the mundane or trivial or unnecessary negative stuff. We brush aside all the clutter of the low quality to make more room for the truly important.

Would you bother with the things that normally bother you if it meant less time with those you love? You'd give up battling the wrong and you'd want only to make more right. You'd stop complaining about your loved ones' faults and would only want to show your appreciation and gratitude.

Impending death reliably brings words of love. An awareness of death heightens your motivation to go on adventures, do great works, take long, sweet, deep breaths of air.

Death separates chaff from grain, the unimportant from the dear. Death wakes us up and says, "Live while you can!" So a palpable awareness of the inevitability of death brings the sweetest life.

Wouldn't you like to have that kind of aliveness without having to die soon?

What prevents it? The *fear* of death is one thing that prevents it. We don't want to think about death because it is a horrible thought. When we die, we leave the people we love. That's one of the greatest horrors of death: We lose the ones we love.

But if you can face up to the bad part, you get the rewards of the good part.

So confront it. Be with it. *Feel* it. Because here's the thing: Death approaches! Death always approaches.

Now, while your death seems years away, you sort of pretend it doesn't exist. But even if it is *years* away, it is still there waiting for you at the end of the track and every day it's closer.

And without a doubt, the moment will come when death is so close you have no choice but to face it.

I say better sooner than later. Better to live fully between now and death rather than live fully in the few seconds between the realization of imminent death and death itself.

But to do that, you have to face the horror.

People want to avoid thinking about death, but death comes no matter what you do — and since it brings an increased ability to live — it makes good sense to dwell on it. Live like you were dying.

This is a great motto: *Live! Death approaches!*

An awareness of death gives you the motivation to do what you've always wanted to do. It gives you courage.

Facing death empowers us and heightens our senses. The horror of the separation of the ultimate end creates great joy at being alive. It is the ultimate comparison reframe. It puts us in touch with the rapture of embracing the people we love.

So don't avoid thoughts of death — but rather remind yourself your death is guaranteed. Feel it. *Feel* the inevitability of it. *Feel* the horror of it. And then open your eyes and realize you are now alive.

Live! Death approaches.

It's not morbid to stay aware of your inevitable death. It's magical.

The sooner you become aware of death, the sooner you get to turn up the volume on life. Death counsels life. Connected to death, we gain the power to really live.

ABOUT THE AUTHORS

Adam Khan is the creator and webmaster of the web site, youmeworks.com. He blogs at moodraiser.com, and he's the author of the books, *Self-Help Stuff That Works*, *Principles For Personal Growth* (now being used as a textbook for a college course in San Diego), *What Difference Does It Make: How the Sexes Differ and What You Can Do About It*, *Direct Your Mind*, *Cultivating Fire: How to Keep Your Motivation White Hot*, *Antivirus For Your Mind*, *Slotralogy*, and *Self-Reliance, Translated*.

Adam has been published in *Prevention Magazine*, *Cosmopolitan*, *Body Bulletin*, *Your Personal Best Newsletter*, *Wisdom*, *Think and Grow Rich Newsletter*, the *Success Strategies* newsletter, and he was a regular columnist for *At Your Best* (a Rodale Press publication) for seven years where his monthly column was voted the readers' favorite. You can write to him at adamkhan@usa.com.

Klassy Evans began conducting communication seminars and workshops in the business and private sector in 1982. She is also the creator of the seminars, *The Happiness Course* and *How to Handle People Who Bring You Down*. And she is the editor of *Self-Help Stuff That Works* and *Principles For Personal Growth*. Write to her at klassy@usa.com.

CPSIA information can be obtained
at www.ICGtesting.com
Printed in the USA
LVOW11s1311111017
551986LV00038B/4/P